TEACHER APPROVED!

Get Ready For
Kindergarten

294 ACTIVITIES AND 2,186 ILLUSTRATIONS

BLACK DOG
& LEVENTHAL
PUBLISHERS
NEW YORK

ISBN 978-1-57912-868-5

Library of Congress Cataloging-in-Publication Data on file
at the offices of Black Dog & Leventhal Publishers, Inc.

Manufactured in China

Published by
Black Dog & Leventhal Publishers, Inc.
151 West 19th Street
New York, New York 10011

Distributed by
Workman Publishing Company
225 Varick Street
New York, New York 10014

h g f e

Contents

A Note to Parents

Get Ready for Kindergarten is an indispensable educational companion for your pre-kindergarten child. It is chock full of fun, interesting, curriculum-based activities—such as those focusing on the alphabet, numbers, colors, shapes, math readiness, nature, and more—that will introduce your child to new concepts while reinforcing what he or she already knows. In addition, there are plenty of fun word games, mazes, and coloring activities that are designed to entertain and amuse your child while boosting his or her basic skills.

In the back of the book you will find a Suggested Reading List. We recommend setting aside some time each day to read with your child. The more your child reads, the faster he or she will acquire other skills. We also suggest that you have your child complete a portion of the book each day. You and your child can sit down and discuss what the goals for each day will be, and perhaps even choose a reward to be given upon completion of the whole book—such as a trip to the park, a special play date, or something else that seems appropriate to you. While you want to help your child set educational goals, be sure to offer lots of encouragement along the way. These activities are not meant as a test. By making them fun and rewarding, you will help your child look forward to completing them, and he or she will be especially eager to tackle the educational challenges ahead! ★

**Hey Kids!
Remember to have
a pencil and
some crayons
handy when
playing with your
Get Ready book!**

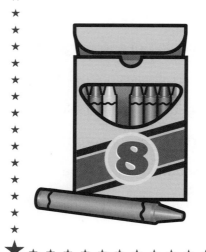

Start here...

FROM

A

TO

The Alphabet

Z

...End here

★ 9 ★

The Alphabet

Point to each letter of the **alphabet** and say it out loud. What words can you name that begin with that letter?

A a B b C c D d

E e F f G g H h

I i J j K k L l M m

N n O o P p Q q

R r S s T t U u V v

W w X x Y y Z z

Beginning Sounds

Can you figure out the first letter of each picture? Write it on the line.

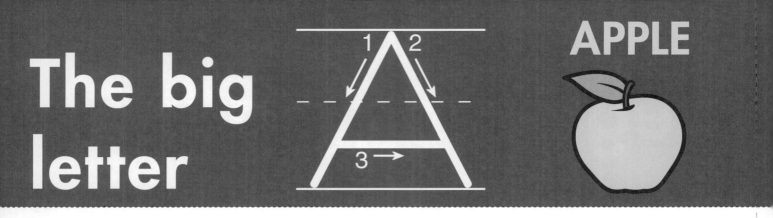

The big letter

APPLE

This is the uppercase **A**. Use your finger to trace it.
Now practice writing the uppercase **A** by following the arrows.

ARTIST

The little letter

ant

This is the lowercase **a**. Use your finger to trace it.
Now practice writing the lowercase **a** by following the arrows.

Practice writing both the upper-case **A** and lowercase **a** on a separate piece of paper.

The big letter B

This is the uppercase **B**. Use your finger to trace it.
Now practice writing the uppercase **B** by following the arrows.

BALLERINA

The little letter

This is the lowercase **b**. Use your finger to trace it.
Now practice writing the lowercase **b** by following the arrows.

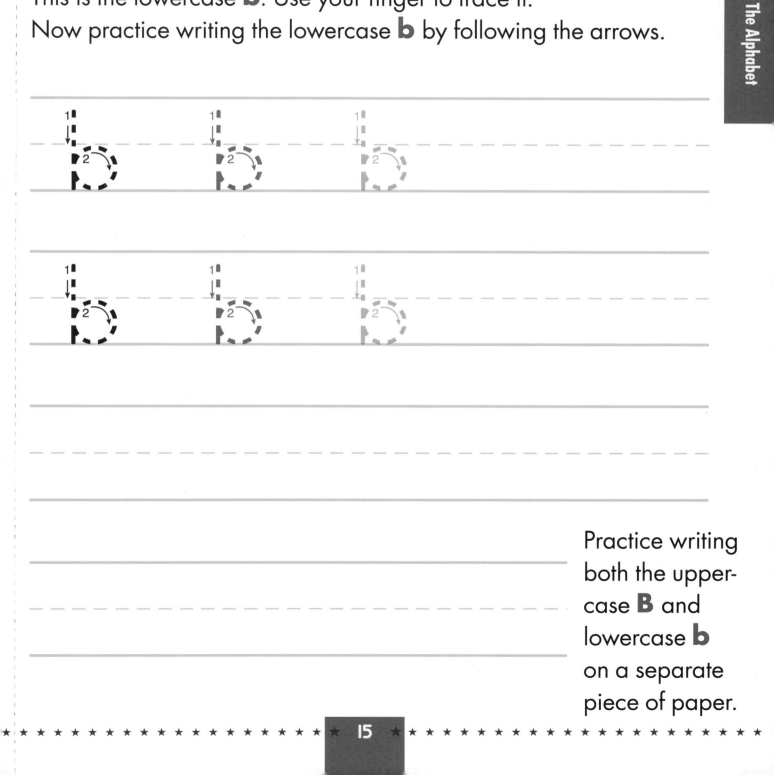

Practice writing both the upper-case **B** and lowercase **b** on a separate piece of paper.

15

The big letter C

This is the uppercase **C**. Use your finger to trace it.
Now practice writing the uppercase **C** by following the arrows.

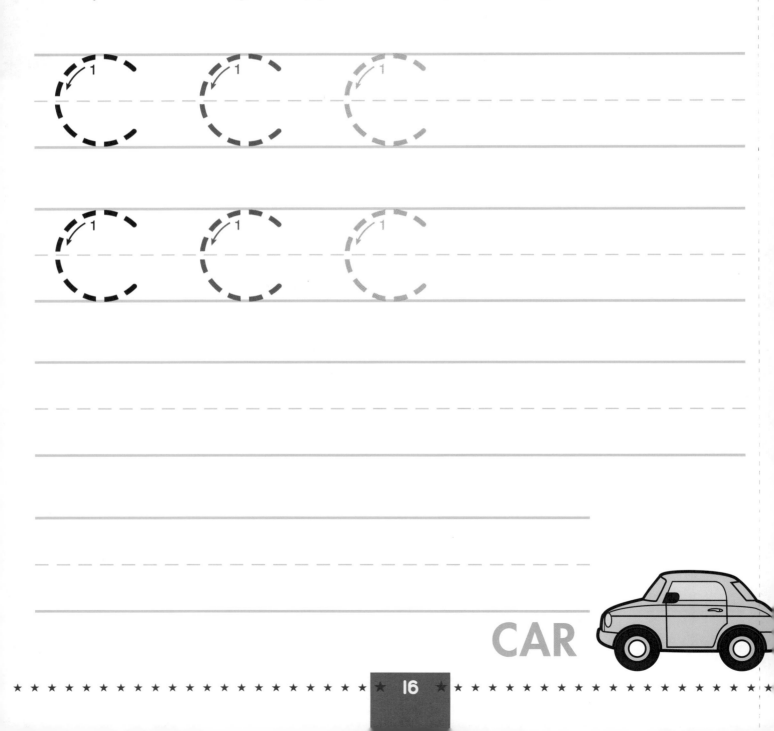

CAR

The little letter

This is the lowercase **c**. Use your finger to trace it.
Now practice writing the lowercase **c** by following the arrows.

Practice writing both the upper-case **C** and lowercase **c** on a separate piece of paper.

The big letter D

This is the uppercase **D**. Use your finger to trace it.
Now practice writing the uppercase **D** by following the arrows.

DENTIST

The little letter

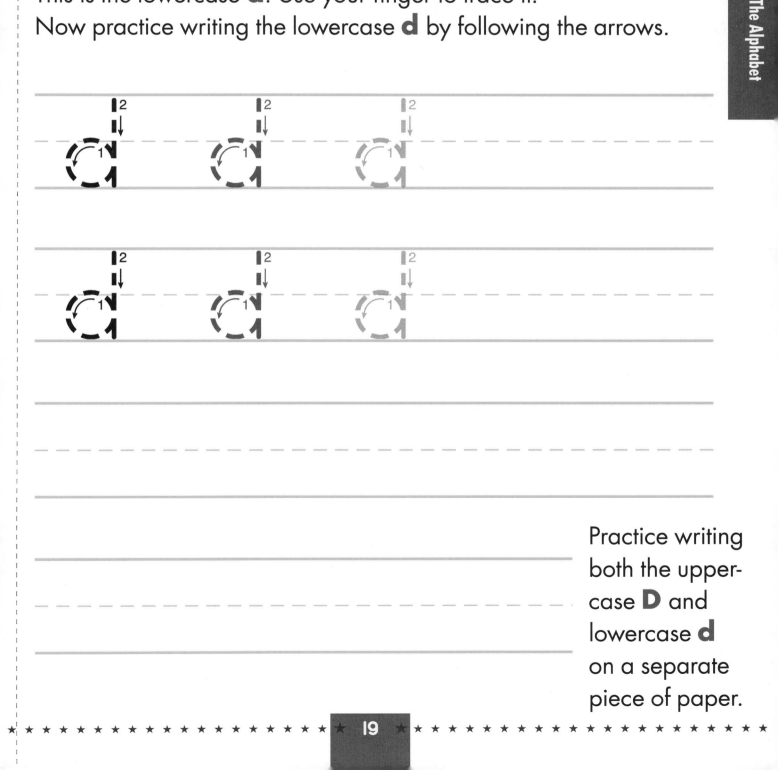

drum

This is the lowercase **d**. Use your finger to trace it.
Now practice writing the lowercase **d** by following the arrows.

Practice writing both the upper-case **D** and lowercase **d** on a separate piece of paper.

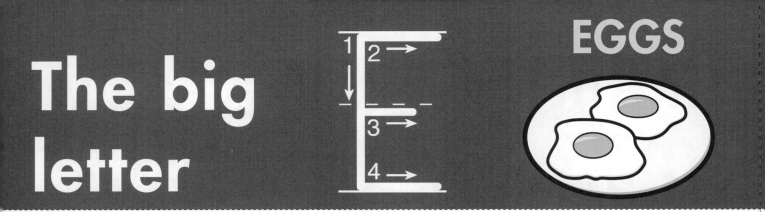

The big letter

EGGS

This is the uppercase **E**. Use your finger to trace it.
Now practice writing the uppercase **E** by following the arrows.

ELEPHANT

The little letter e

This is the lowercase **e**. Use your finger to trace it.
Now practice writing the lowercase **e** by following the arrows.

Practice writing both the upper-case **E** and lowercase **e** on a separate piece of paper.

The big letter

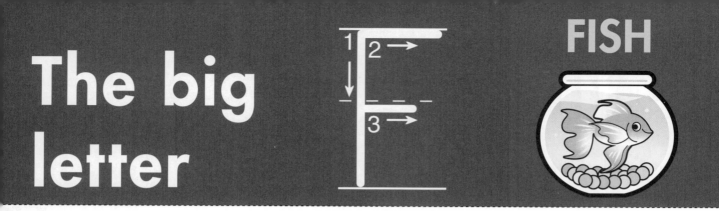

This is the uppercase **F**. Use your finger to trace it.

Now practice writing the uppercase **F** by following the arrows.

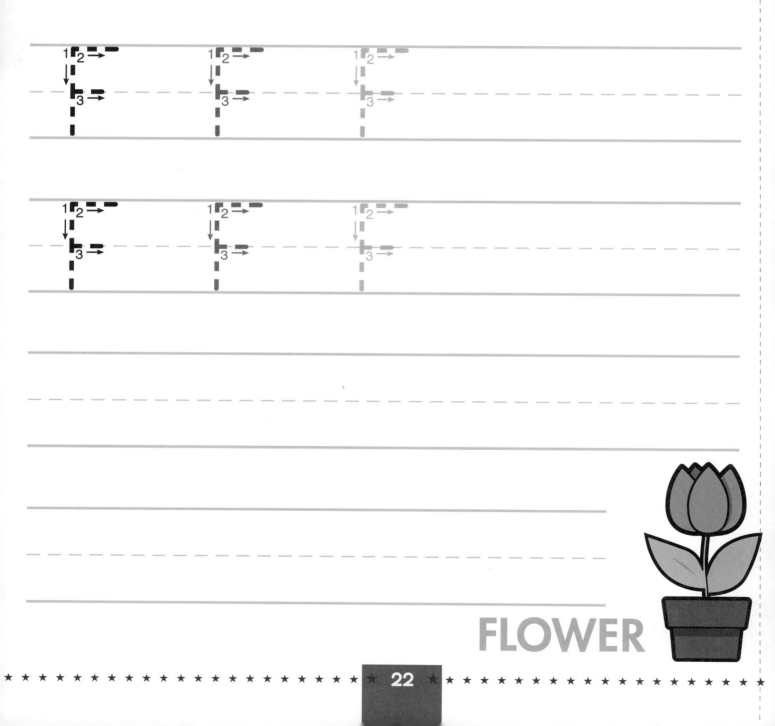

FLOWER

The little letter

football

This is the lowercase **f**. Use your finger to trace it.
Now practice writing the lowercase **f** by following the arrows.

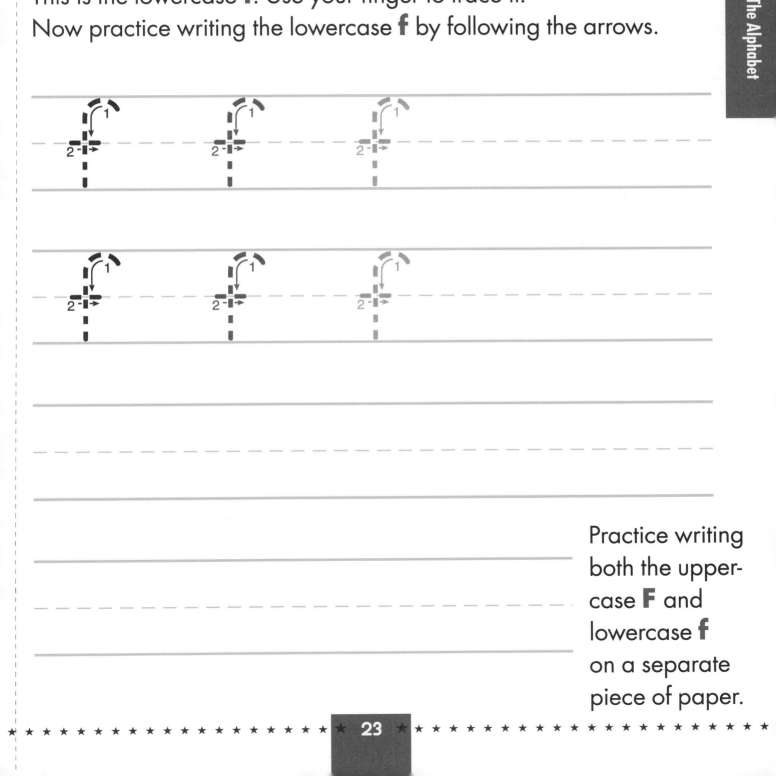

Practice writing both the upper-case **F** and lowercase **f** on a separate piece of paper.

The big letter

GOAT

This is the uppercase **G**. Use your finger to trace it.
Now practice writing the uppercase **G** by following the arrows.

GORILLA

The little letter g

This is the lowercase **g**. Use your finger to trace it.
Now practice writing the lowercase **g** by following the arrows.

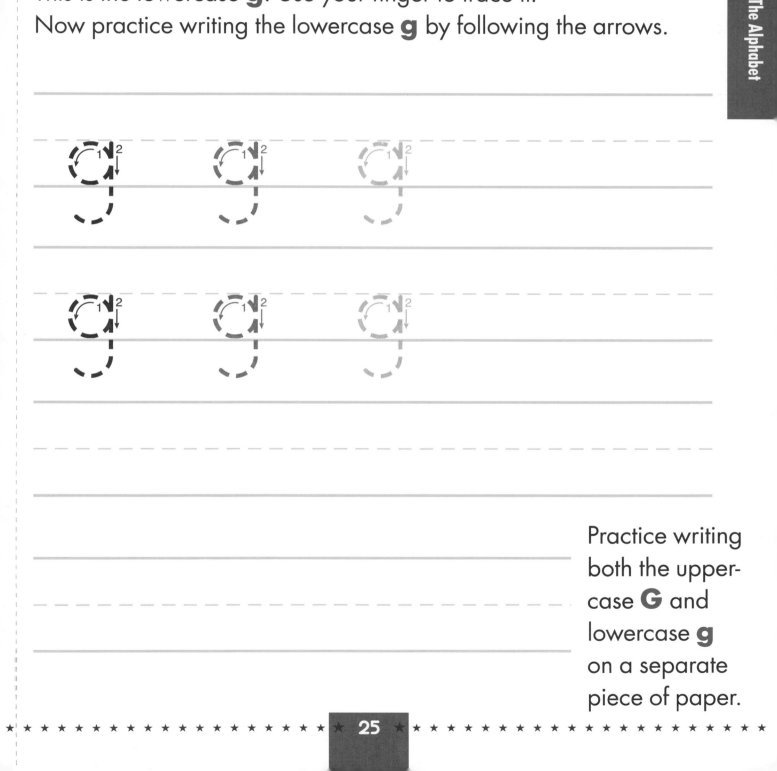

Practice writing both the upper-case **G** and lowercase **g** on a separate piece of paper.

The big letter

This is the uppercase **H**. Use your finger to trace it.
Now practice writing the uppercase **H** by following the arrows.

HAMSTER

The little letter h

helicopter

This is the lowercase **h**. Use your finger to trace it.
Now practice writing the lowercase **h** by following the arrows.

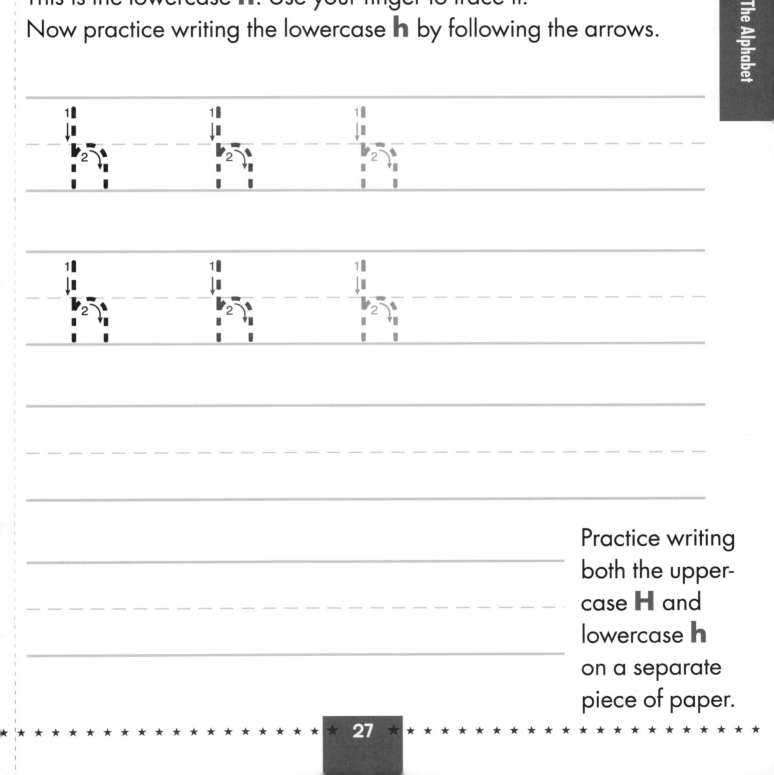

Practice writing both the upper-case **H** and lowercase **h** on a separate piece of paper.

The big letter

This is the uppercase **I**. Use your finger to trace it.
Now practice writing the uppercase **I** by following the arrows.

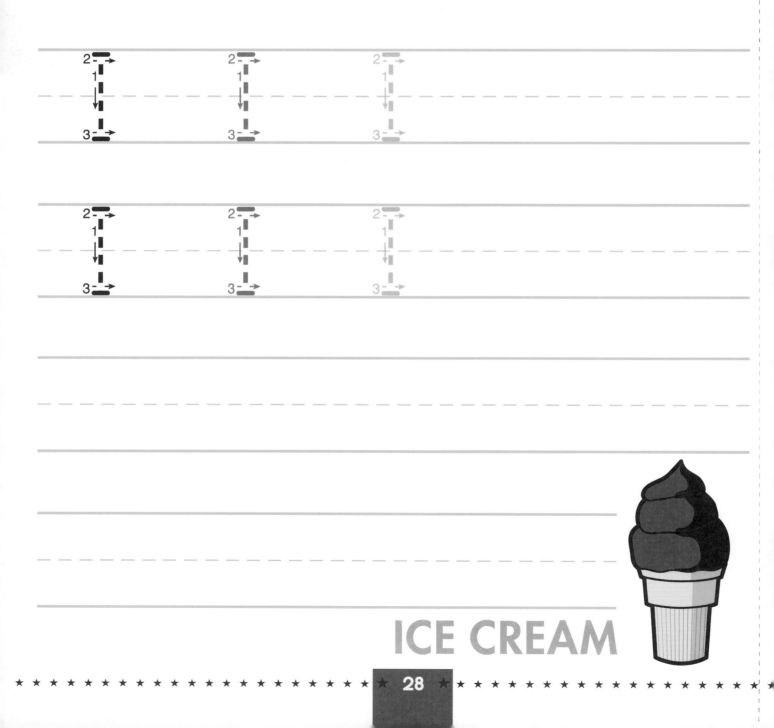

ICE CREAM

The little letter

insect

This is the lowercase **i**. Use your finger to trace it.
Now practice writing the lowercase **i** by following the arrows.

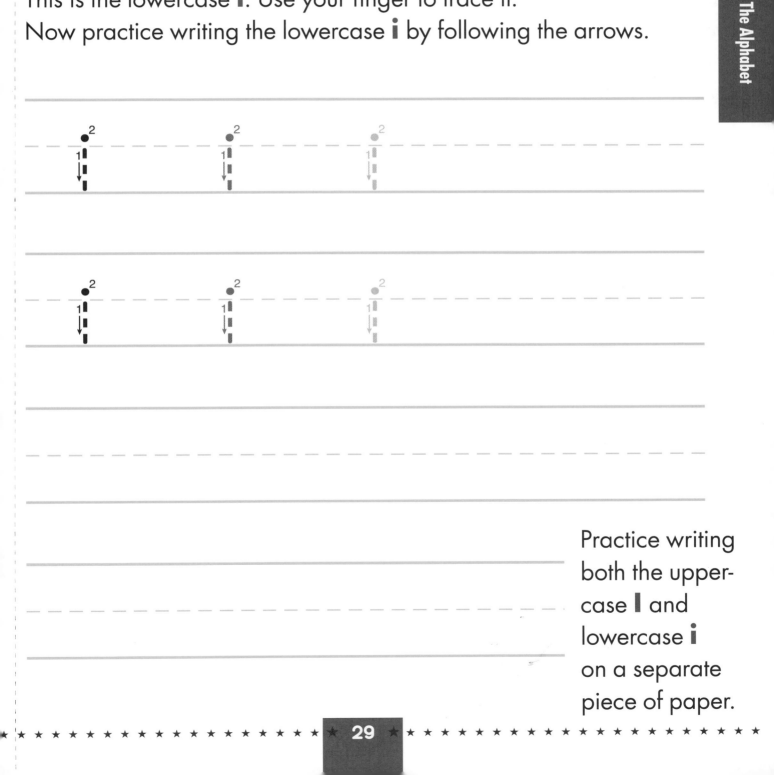

Practice writing both the upper-case **I** and lowercase **i** on a separate piece of paper.

The big letter

This is the uppercase **J**. Use your finger to trace it.
Now practice writing the uppercase **J** by following the arrows.

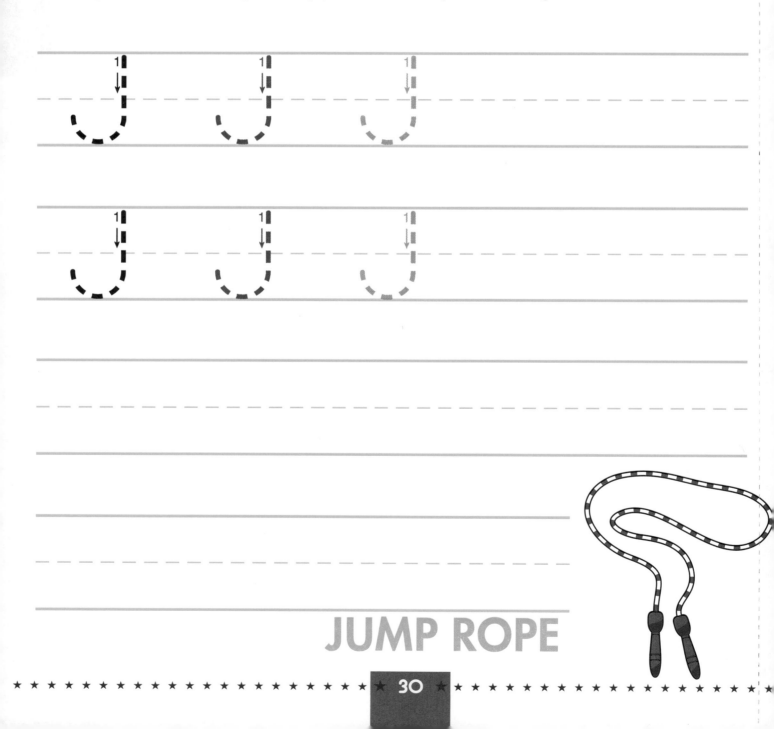

JUMP ROPE

JACK

The little letter j

jeans

This is the lowercase **j**. Use your finger to trace it.
Now practice writing the lowercase **j** by following the arrows.

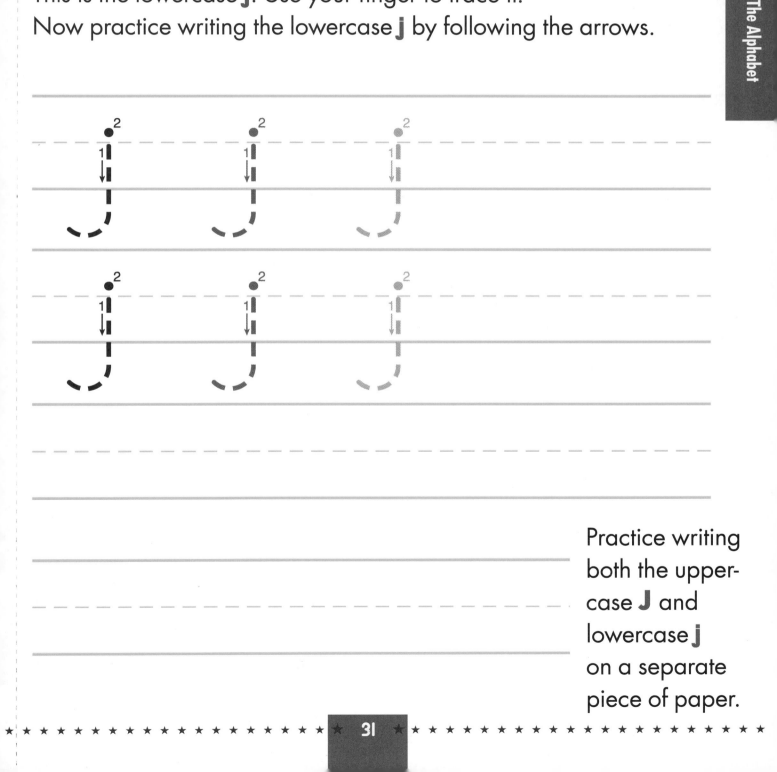

Practice writing both the upper-case **J** and lowercase **j** on a separate piece of paper.

The big letter

KITE

This is the uppercase **K**. Use your finger to trace it.
Now practice writing the uppercase **K** by following the arrows.

KANGAROO

The little letter

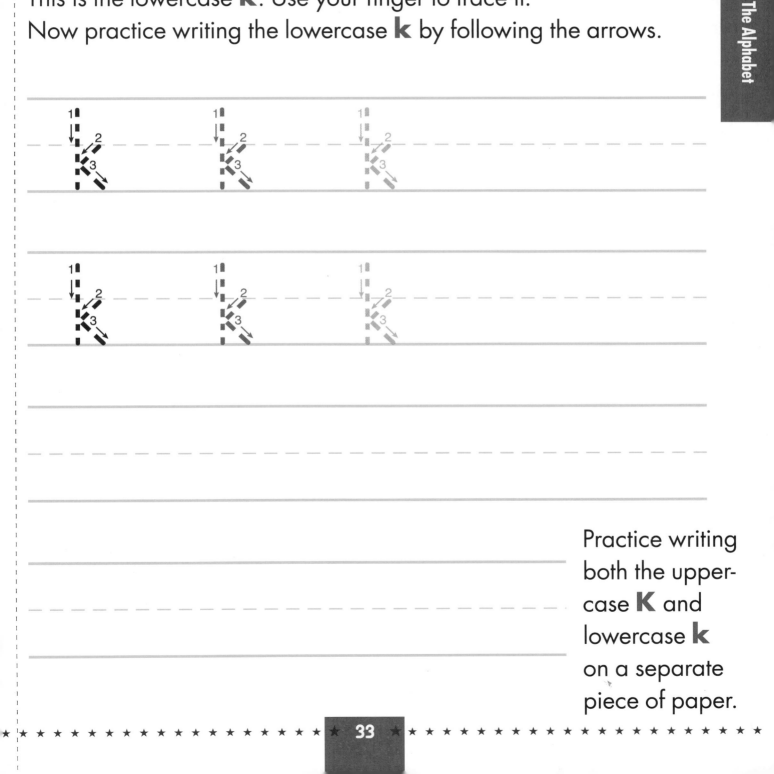

koala

This is the lowercase **k**. Use your finger to trace it.
Now practice writing the lowercase **k** by following the arrows.

Practice writing both the uppercase **K** and lowercase **k** on a separate piece of paper.

The big letter

This is the uppercase **L**. Use your finger to trace it.
Now practice writing the uppercase **L** by following the arrows.

LADYBUG

The little letter

leaf

This is the lowercase **l**. Use your finger to trace it.
Now practice writing the lowercase **l** by following the arrows.

Practice writing both the upper-case **L** and lowercase **l** on a separate piece of paper.

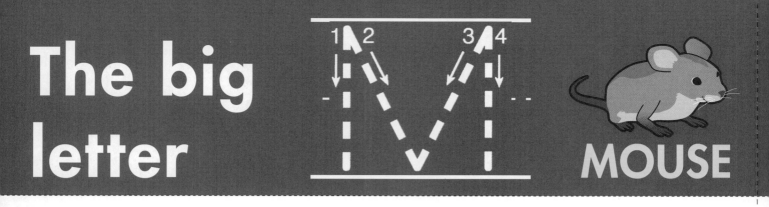

The big letter

MOUSE

This is the uppercase **M**. Use your finger to trace it.
Now practice writing the uppercase **M** by following the arrows.

MONEY

The little letter

mushroom

This is the lowercase **m**. Use your finger to trace it.
Now practice writing the lowercase **m** by following the arrows.

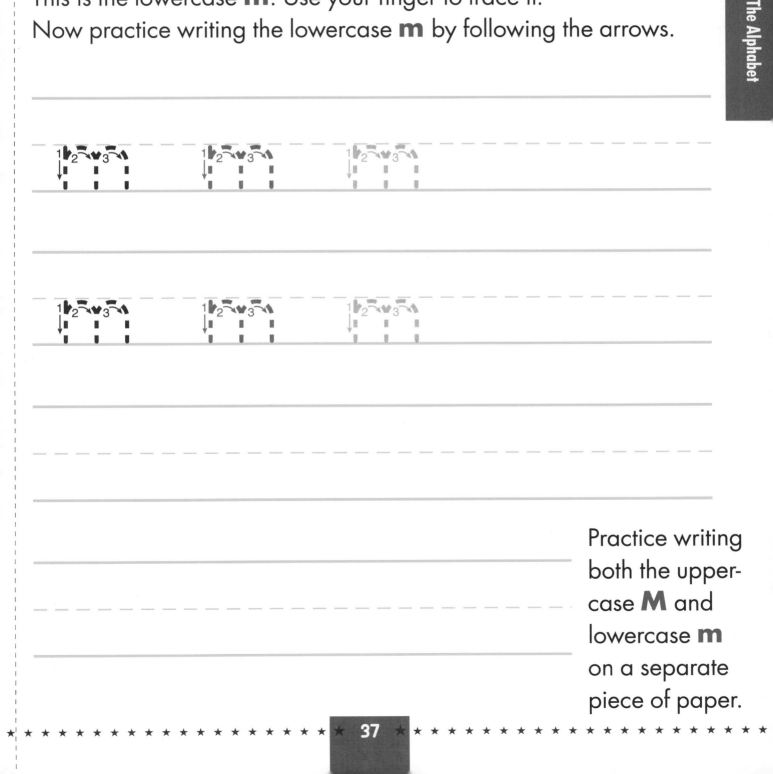

Practice writing both the uppercase **M** and lowercase **m** on a separate piece of paper.

The big letter

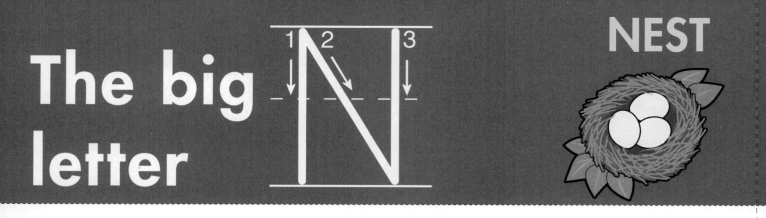

This is the uppercase **N**. Use your finger to trace it.
Now practice writing the uppercase **N** by following the arrows.

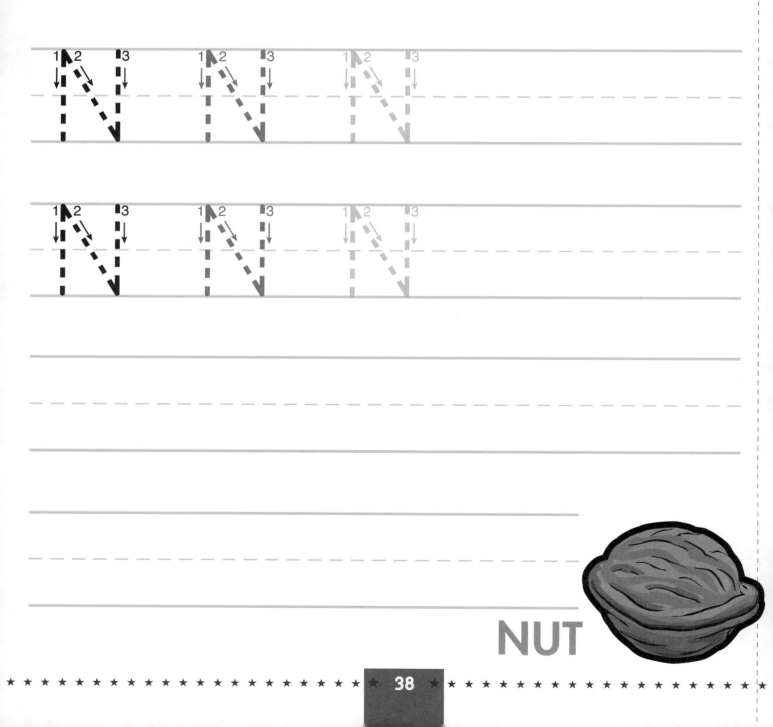

NUT

The little letter

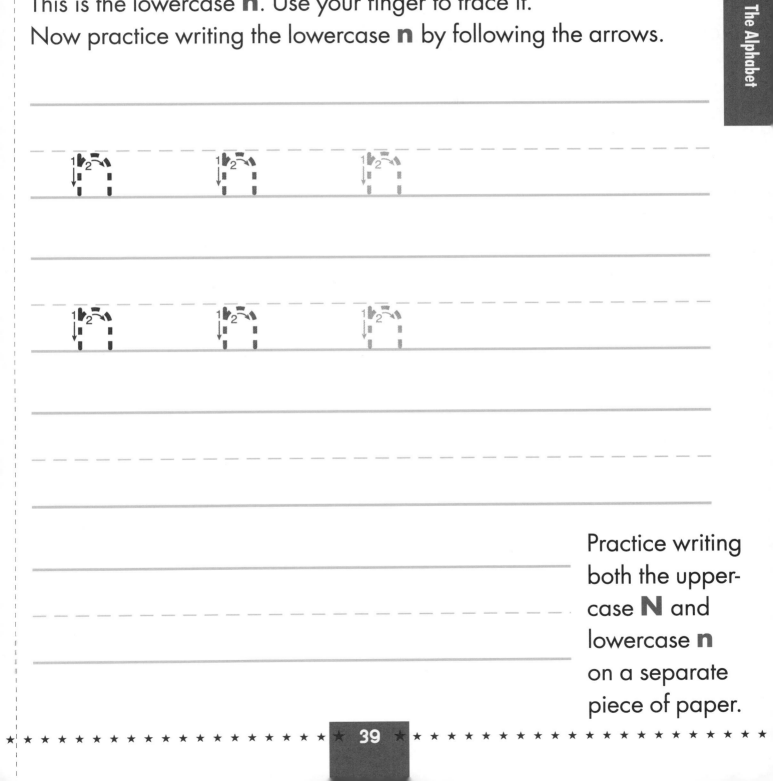

necklace

This is the lowercase **n**. Use your finger to trace it.
Now practice writing the lowercase **n** by following the arrows.

Practice writing both the upper-case **N** and lowercase **n** on a separate piece of paper.

The big letter

This is the uppercase **O**. Use your finger to trace it.
Now practice writing the uppercase **O** by following the arrows.

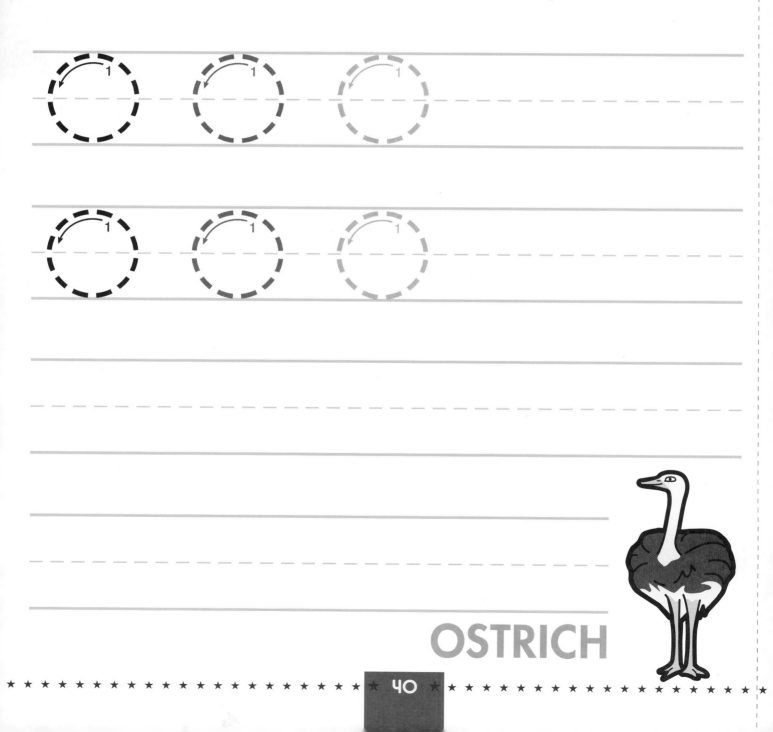

OSTRICH

The little letter

octopus

This is the lowercase o. Use your finger to trace it.
Now practice writing the lowercase o by following the arrows.

Practice writing both the uppercase O and lowercase o on a separate piece of paper.

The big letter

This is the uppercase **P**. Use your finger to trace it.
Now practice writing the uppercase **P** by following the arrows.

PANDA

The little letter p

pumpkin

This is the lowercase **p**. Use your finger to trace it.
Now practice writing the lowercase **p** by following the arrows.

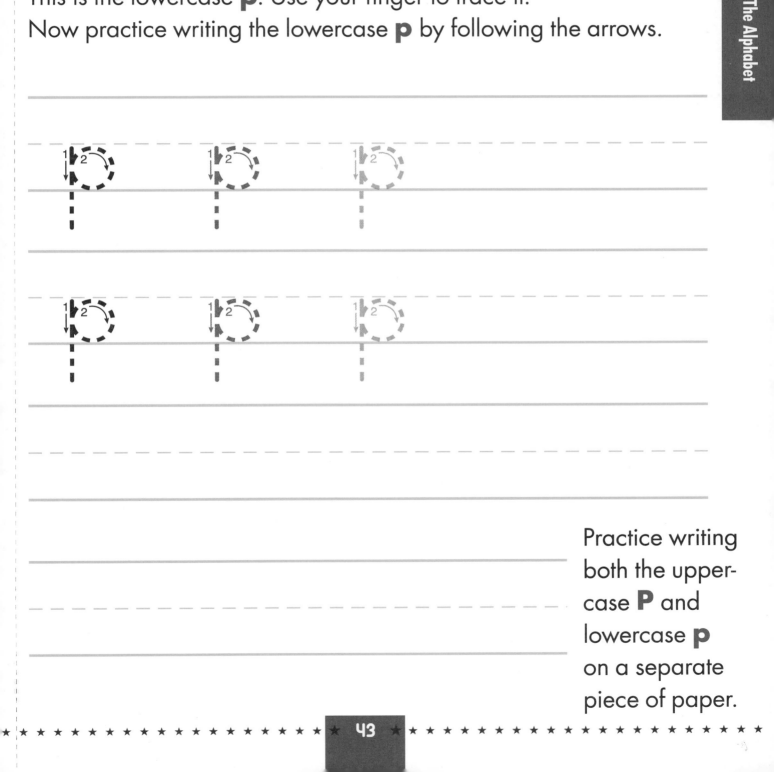

Practice writing both the upper-case **P** and lowercase **p** on a separate piece of paper.

The big letter Q

This is the uppercase **Q**. Use your finger to trace it.
Now practice writing the uppercase **Q** by following the arrows.

QUEEN

The little letter

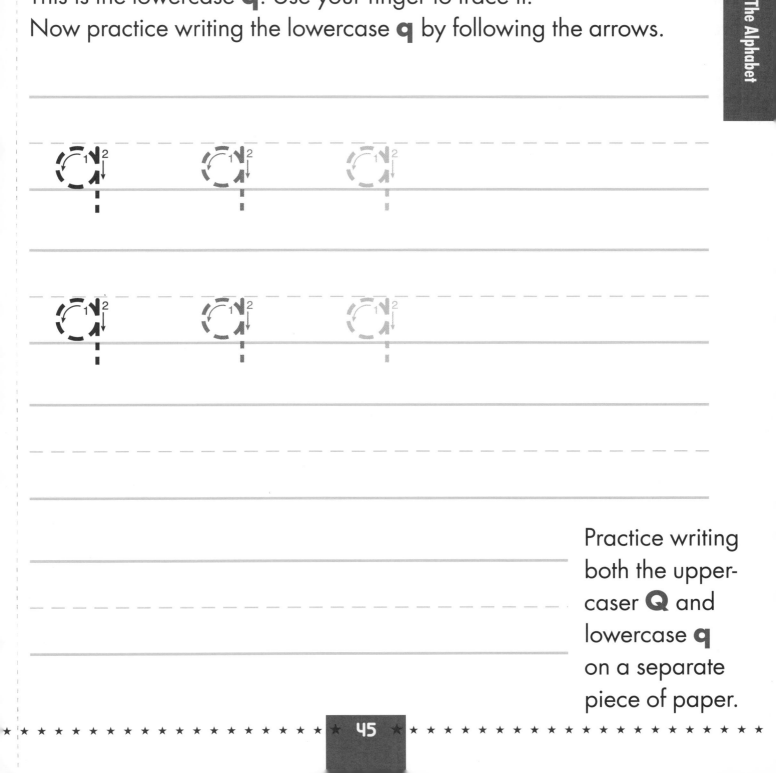

quail

This is the lowercase **q**. Use your finger to trace it.
Now practice writing the lowercase **q** by following the arrows.

Practice writing both the upper-caser **Q** and lowercase **q** on a separate piece of paper.

The big letter

RHINO

This is the uppercase **R**. Use your finger to trace it.
Now practice writing the uppercase **R** by following the arrows.

ROBOT

The little letter

rabbit

This is the lowercase **r**. Use your finger to trace it.
Now practice writing the lowercase **r** by following the arrows.

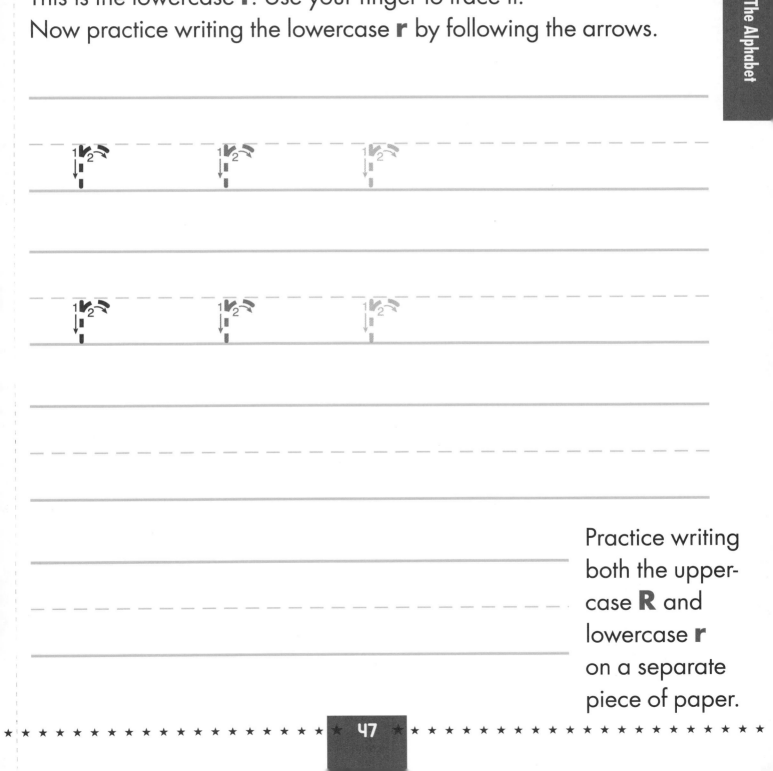

Practice writing
both the upper-
case **R** and
lowercase **r**
on a separate
piece of paper.

The big letter

This is the uppercase **S**. Use your finger to trace it.
Now practice writing the uppercase **S** by following the arrows.

SHEEP

The little letter

s

shoes

This is the lowercase **s**. Use your finger to trace it.
Now practice writing the lowercase **s** by following the arrows.

Practice writing both the upper-case **S** and lowercase **s** on a separate piece of paper.

The big letter

This is the uppercase **T**. Use your finger to trace it.
Now practice writing the uppercase **T** by following the arrows.

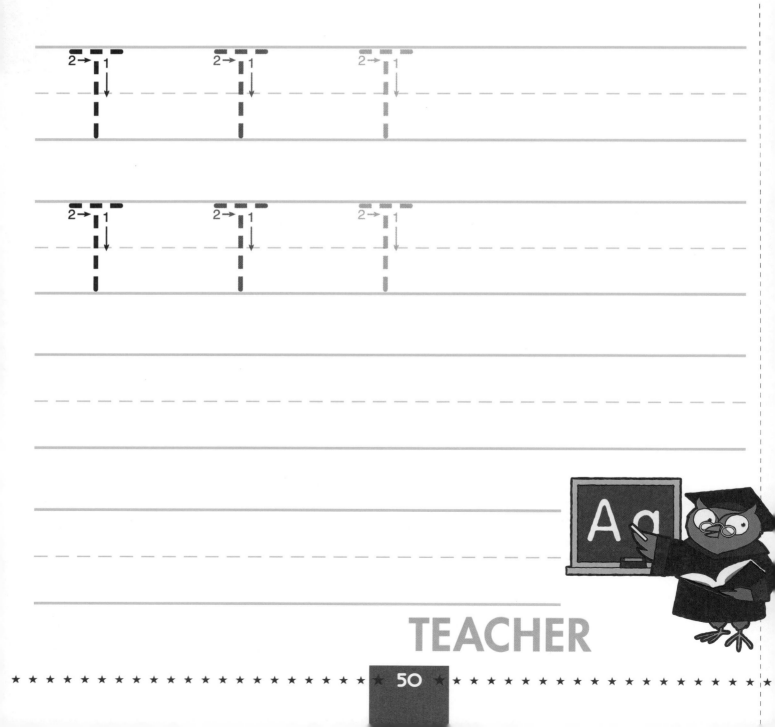

TEACHER

The little letter

tuba

This is the lowercase **t**. Use your finger to trace it.
Now practice writing the lowercase **t** by following the arrows.

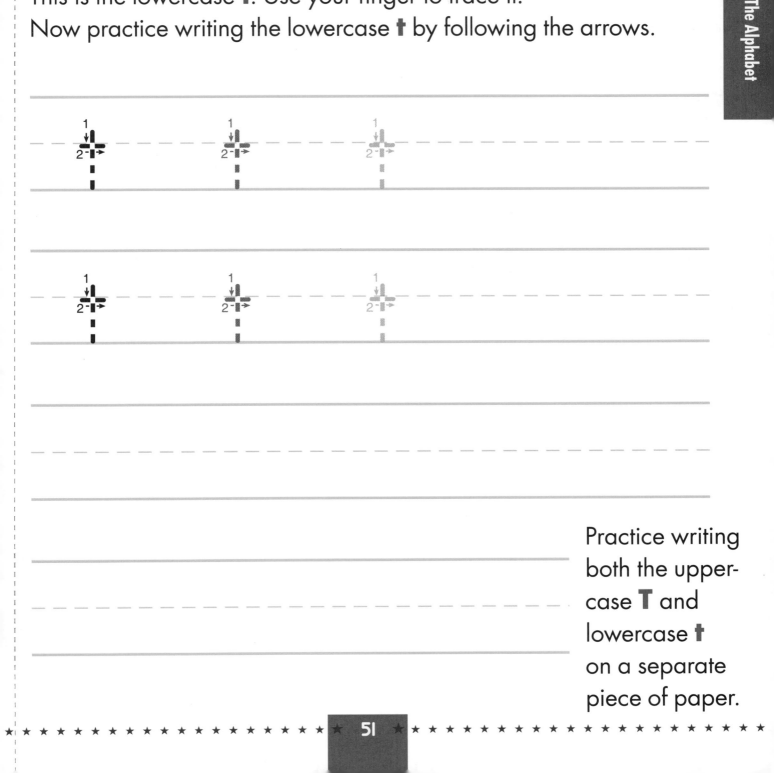

Practice writing both the upper-case **T** and lowercase **t** on a separate piece of paper.

tuba

The big letter U

This is the uppercase **U**. Use your finger to trace it.
Now practice writing the uppercase **U** by following the arrows.

UMBRELLA

The little letter u

uniform

14

This is the lowercase **u**. Use your finger to trace it.
Now practice writing the lowercase **u** by following the arrows.

Practice writing both the upper-case **U** and lowercase **u** on a separate piece of paper.

The big letter V

This is the uppercase **V**. Use your finger to trace it.
Now practice writing the uppercase **V** by following the arrows.

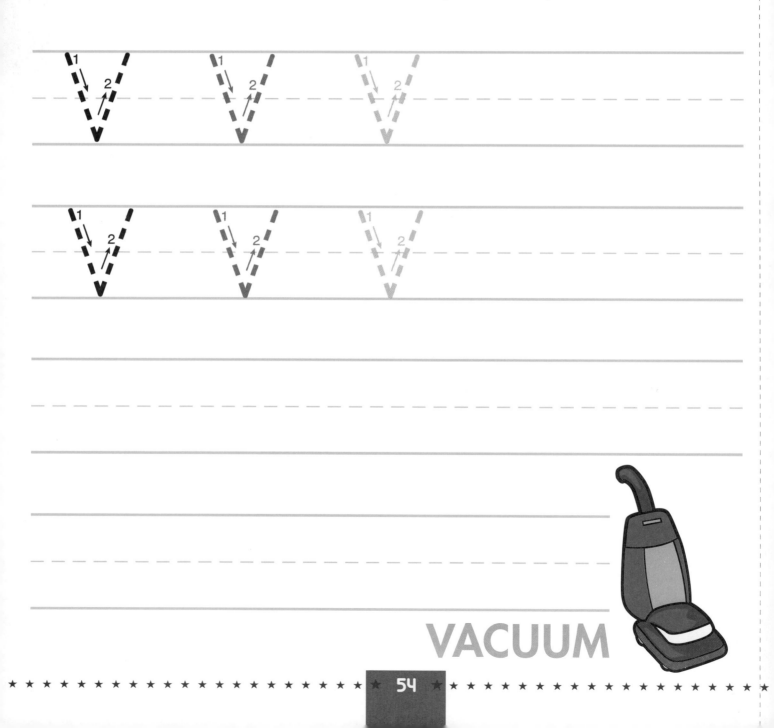

VACUUM

The little letter v

violin

This is the lowercase **v**. Use your finger to trace it.
Now practice writing the lowercase **v** by following the arrows.

Practice writing both the upper-case **V** and lowercase **v** on a separate piece of paper.

The big letter

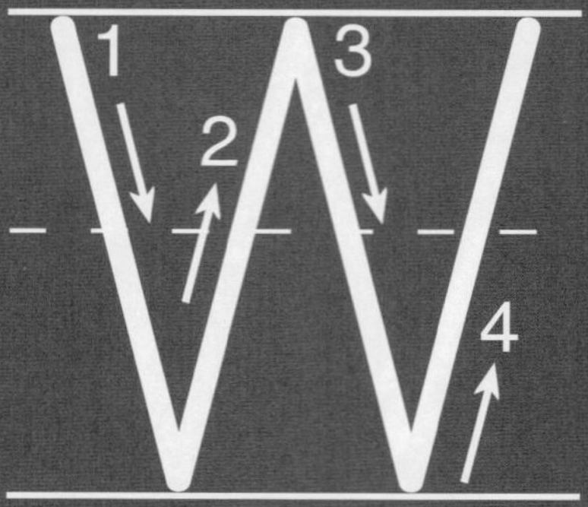

W

This is the uppercase **W**. Use your finger to trace it.
Now practice writing the uppercase **W** by following the arrows.

WAGON

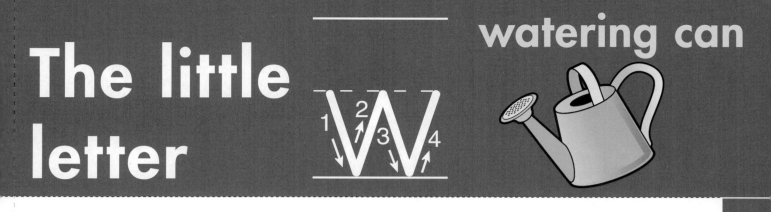

The little letter

watering can

This is the lowercase **w**. Use your finger to trace it.
Now practice writing the lowercase **w** by following the arrows.

Practice writing both the upper-case **W** and lowercase **w** on a separate piece of paper.

The big letter

This is the uppercase **X**. Use your finger to trace it.
Now practice writing the uppercase **X** by following the arrows.

The little letter

This is the lowercase **x**. Use your finger to trace it.
Now practice writing the lowercase **x** by following the arrows.

Practice writing both the upper-case **X** and lowercase **x** on a separate piece of paper.

The big letter

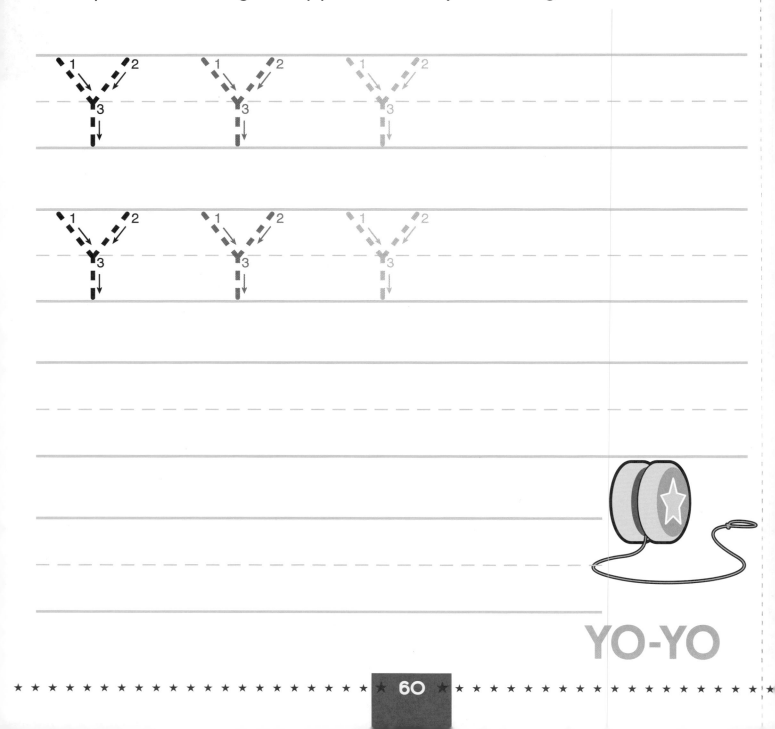

YOGURT

This is the uppercase **Y**. Use your finger to trace it.
Now practice writing the uppercase **Y** by following the arrows.

YO-YO

The little letter

This is the lowercase **y**. Use your finger to trace it.
Now practice writing the lowercase **y** by following the arrows.

Practice writing both the upper-case **Y** and lowercase **y** on a separate piece of paper.

The big letter

This is the uppercase **Z**. Use your finger to trace it.
Now practice writing the uppercase **Z** by following the arrows.

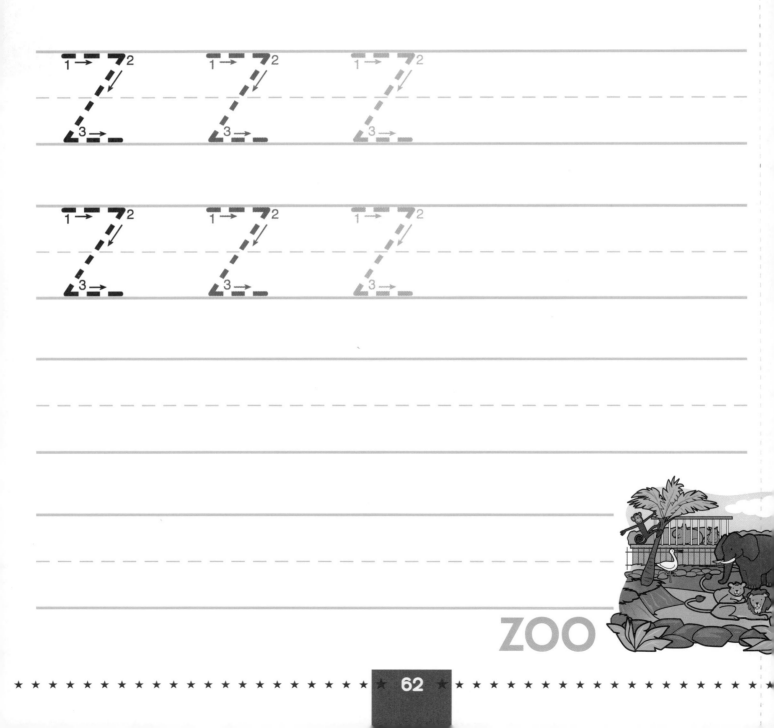

ZOO

The little letter Z

zipper

This is the lowercase **z**. Use your finger to trace it.
Now practice writing the lowercase **z** by following the arrows.

Practice writing both the upper-case **Z** and lowercase **z** on a separate piece of paper.

The Letter D

Each of these squares has a different letter inside it. Color only the squares where you find either the uppercase **D** or lowercase **d**.

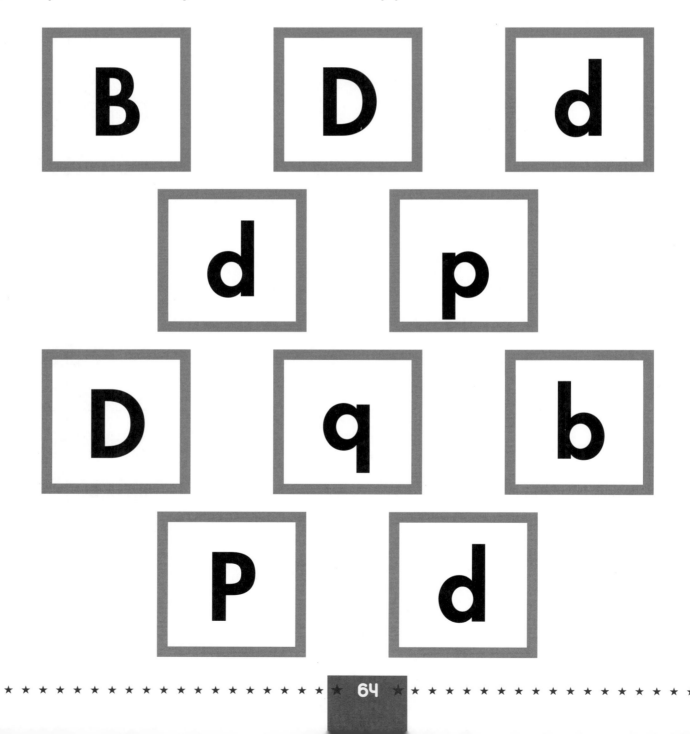

Find the word that begins with F

Which of these two pictures begins with the letter **F**?
Draw a circle around them.

The Letter T

Each of these stars has a different letter inside it. Color only the stars where you find either the uppercase **T** or lowercase **t**.

The Letter S

Circle the three things that begin with the letter **S**.

The Letter Q

Each of these diamonds has a different letter inside it. Color only the diamonds where you find either the uppercase **Q** or lowercase **q**.

The Letter P

Circle the four things that begin with the letter **P**.

The Letter N

Each of these squares has a different letter inside it. Color only the squares where you find either the uppercase **N** or lowercase **n**.

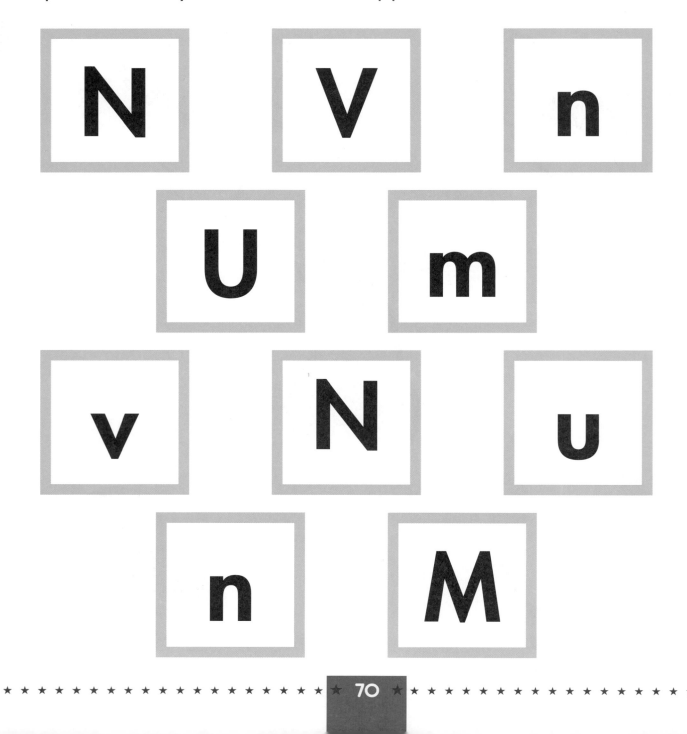

The Letter M

Circle the three things that begin with the letter **M**.

Words that begin with the letter C

C is for Cat. Can you find a cat on this page? Draw a circle around it.

C is for Camel. Where is the camel? Draw a square around it.

C is for Coat. Can you put an X through to the coat on this page?

Uppercase and Lowercase

Draw a line between the uppercase and lowercase letters.

The Letter R

Circle the three things that begin with the letter **R**.

The Letter H

Each of these circles has a different letter inside it. Color only the circles where you find either the uppercase **H** or lowercase **h**.

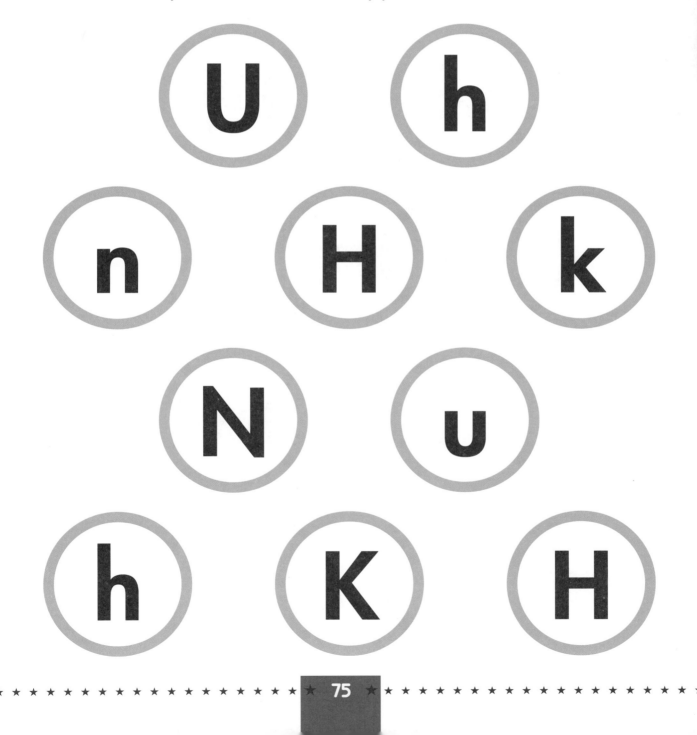

The Letter J

Each of these ovals has a different letter inside it. Color only the ovals where you find either the uppercase **J** or lowercase **j**.

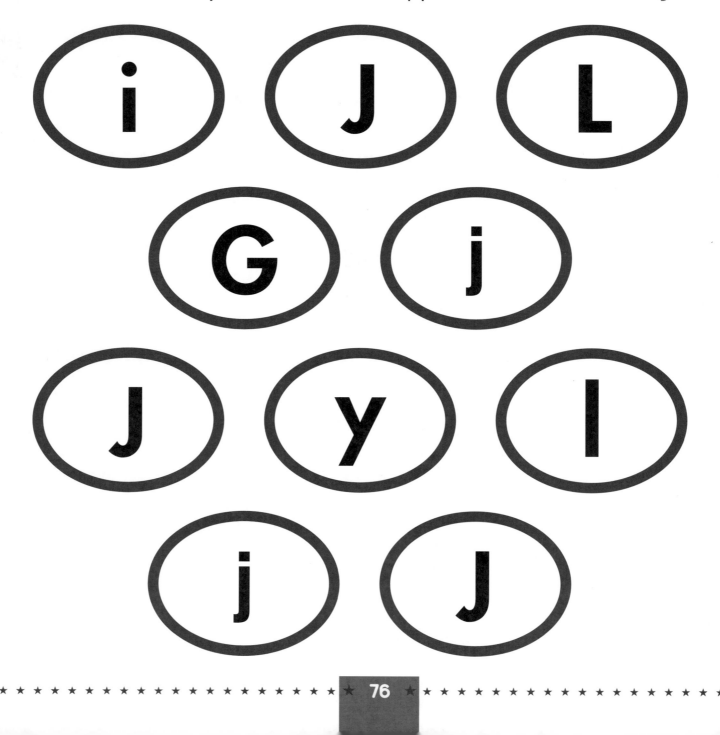

Beginning Sound

Say the name of each picture.
Draw a line to connect each picture on the left
with the picture on the right that begins with the same sound.

P

C

S

The Letter L

Circle the three pictures that begin with the letter **L**.

Words that begin with the letter G

G is for Goat. Can you find a goat on this page? Draw a circle around it.

G is for Grapes. Where are the grapes? Draw a square around them.

G is for Gorilla. Can you put an X through the gorilla on this page?

The Letter W

Each of these squares has a different letter inside it. Color only the squares where you find either the uppercase **W** or lowercase **w**.

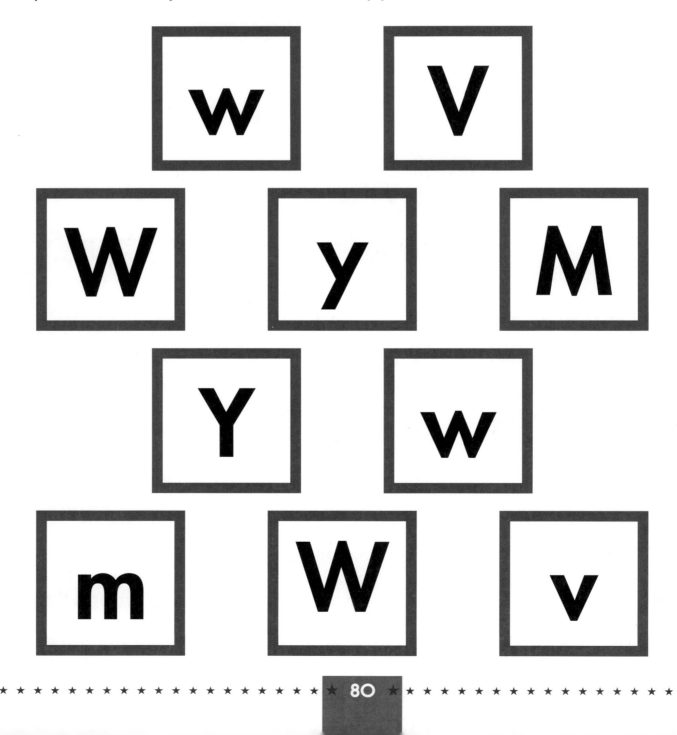

Find the Missing Letters

Fill in the missing letters to complete the words.

do __

__ a t

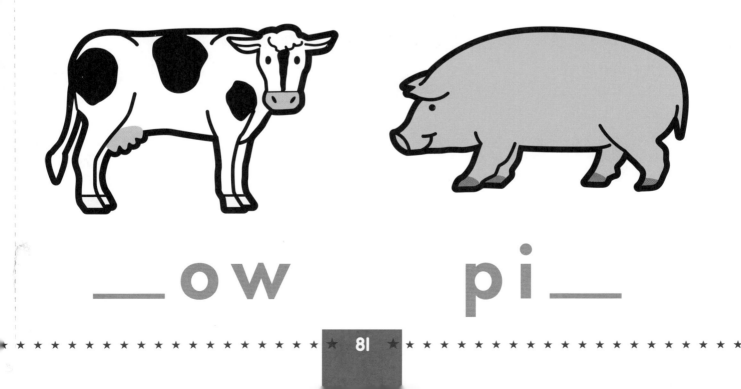

__ o w

pi __

Out of Order

Circle the two places in the uppercase and lowercase alphabet where letters are out of order.

A B C D E F G I H J K L M N
O P Q R S T U V X W Y Z

a c b d e f g h i j k l m n
o p q r s t u v w x y z

IT'S AS

EASY

Numbers
&
Counting

AS

Trace 1-10

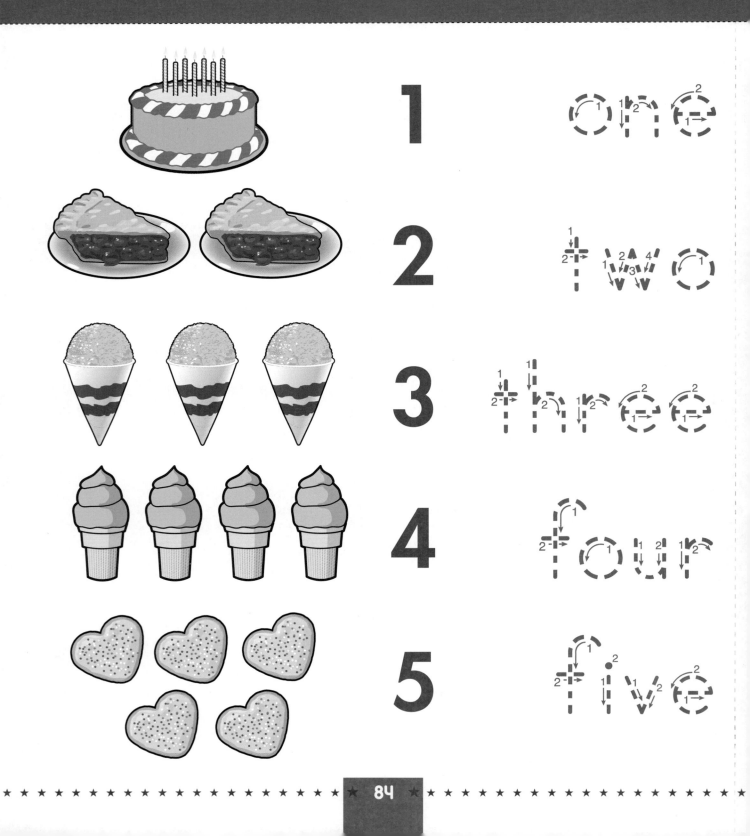

1   one

2   two

3   three

4   four

5   five

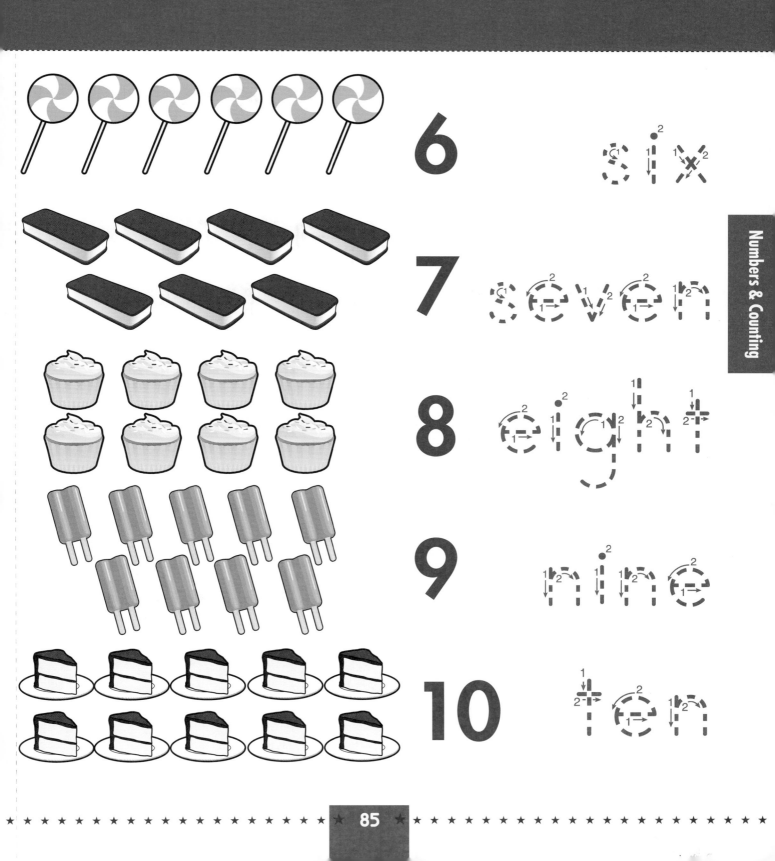

6

seven 7

8 eight

9 nine

10 ten

six

The Number 1 ONE

Color **ONE** barn.

Write the number **ONE** below by following the dotted lines.

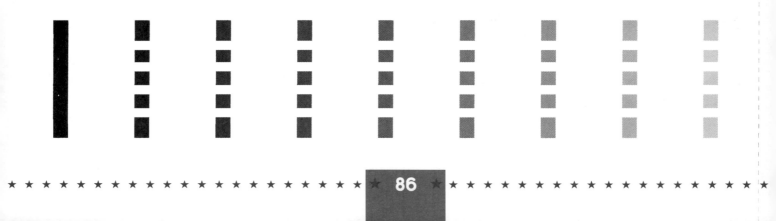

Color **TWO** cows.

Numbers & Counting

Write the number **TWO** below by following the dotted lines.

The Number 3 THREE

Color **THREE** sheep.

Write the number **THREE** below by following the dotted lines.

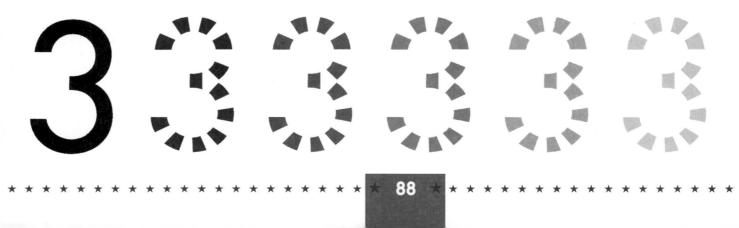

The Number 4 FOUR

Color **FOUR** goats.

Write the number **FOUR** below by following the dotted lines.

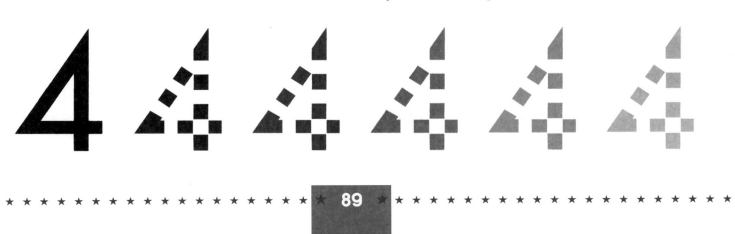

Color **FIVE** horses.

Write the number **FIVE** below by following the dotted lines.

The Number 6

SIX

Color **SIX** pigs.

Write the number **SIX** below by following the dotted lines.

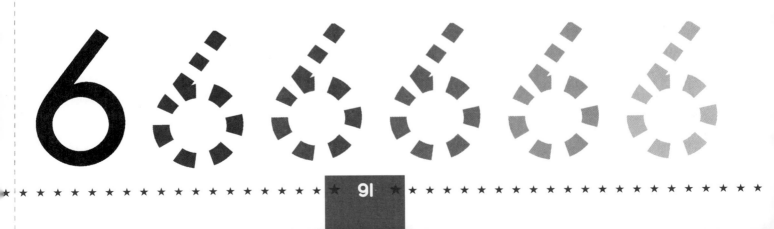

The Number **7** SEVEN

Color **SEVEN** roosters.

Write the number **SEVEN** below by following the dotted lines.

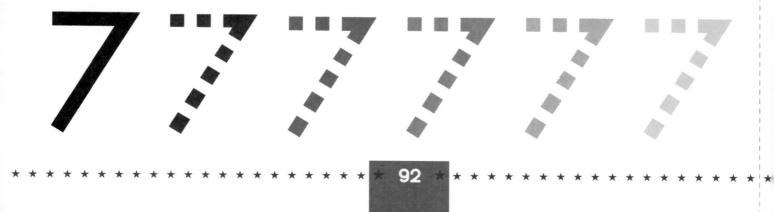

The Number 8 EIGHT

Color **EIGHT** ducks.

Write the number **EIGHT** below by following the dotted lines.

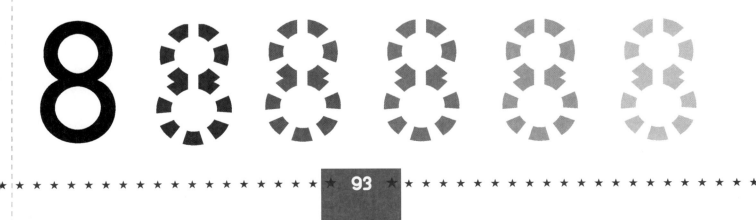

The Number 9 NINE

Color **NINE** chickens.

Write the number **NINE** below by following the dotted lines.

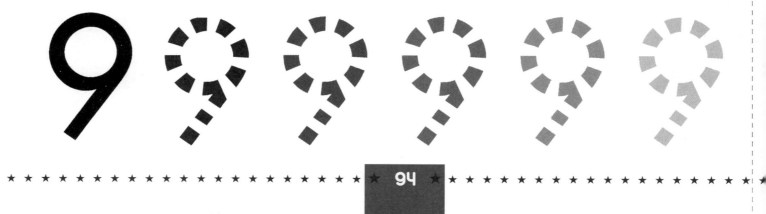

The Number 10 TEN

Color **TEN** chicks.

Numbers & Counting

Write the number **TEN** below by following the dotted lines.

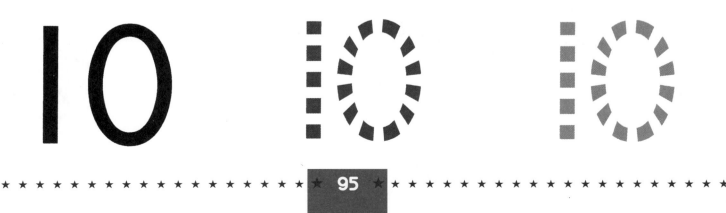

Let's Count to Ten

Fill in the missing numbers.

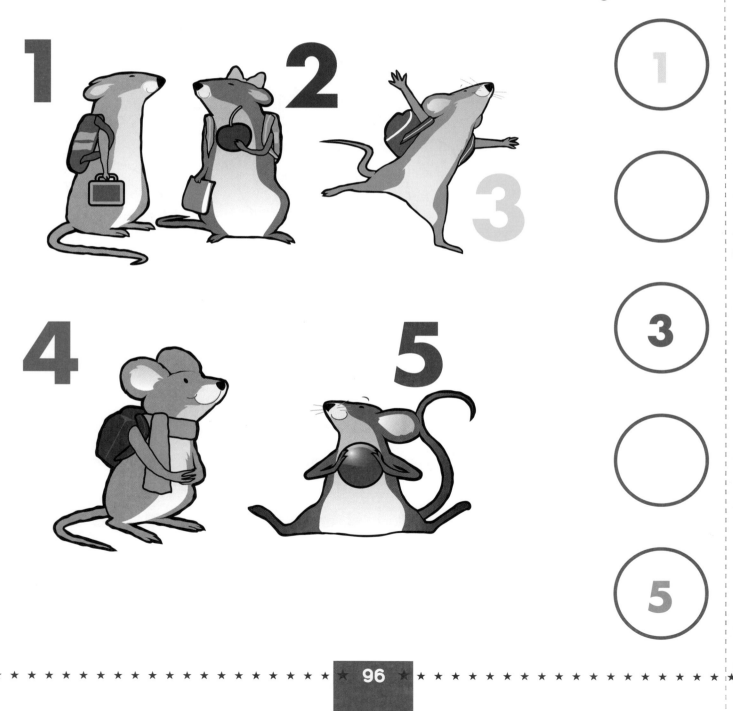

Fill in the missing numbers.

6

7

8

9

10

6

8

10

Play with Numbers

Count each toy and write the correct number in the box.

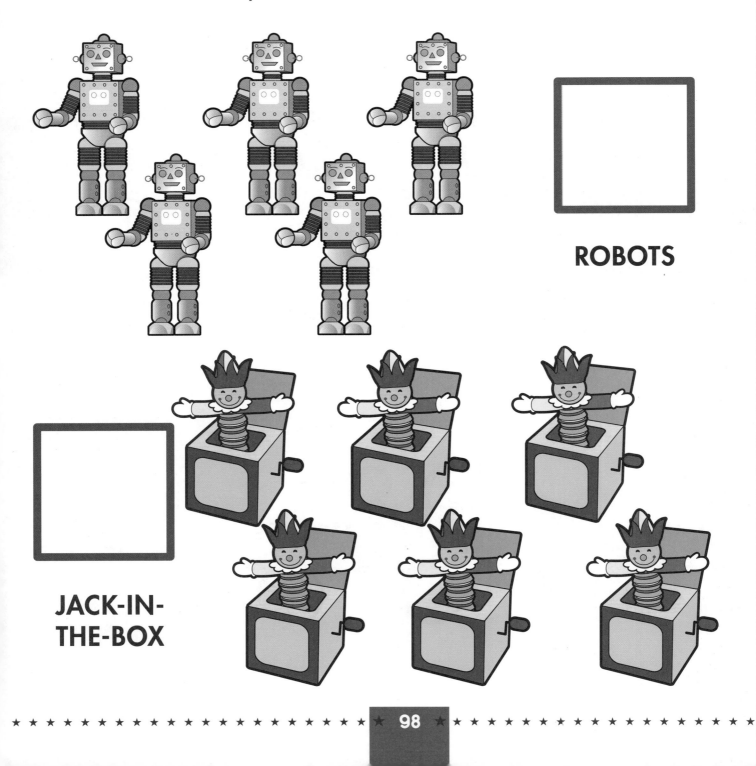

ROBOTS

JACK-IN-THE-BOX

Play with Numbers

Count each toy and write the correct number in the box.

DOLLS

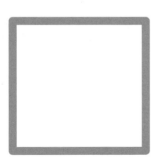

YO-YOS

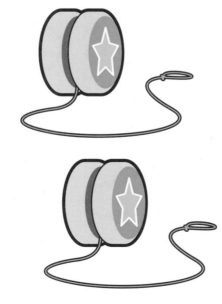

Play with Numbers

Count each toy and write the correct number in the box.

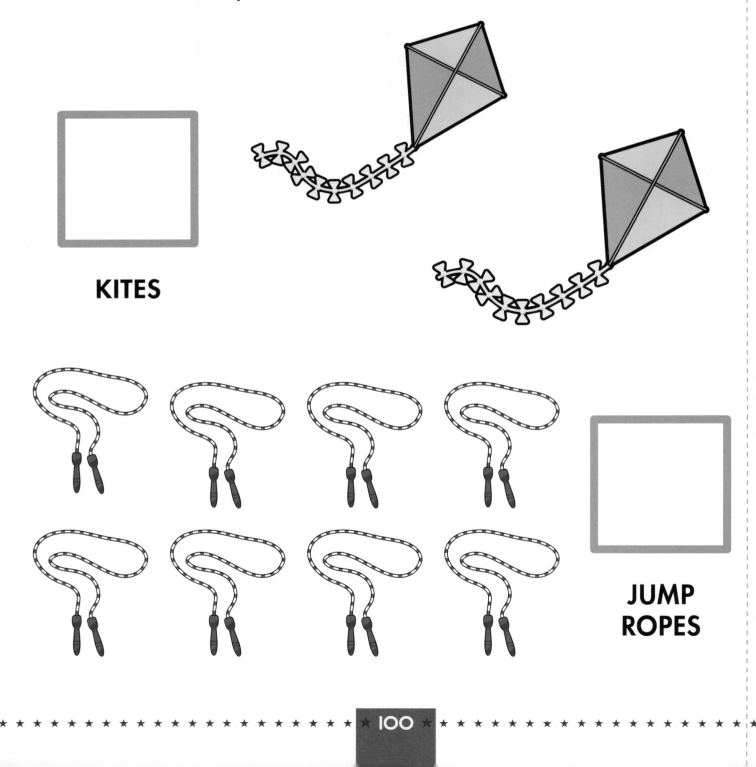

KITES

JUMP
ROPES

Your Fingers

First count all of your fingers. Now place your hand on the page and use a pencil to trace around it.

How many fingers do you have on both hands?

How Many Are There?

Count each bug and write the correct number on the line.

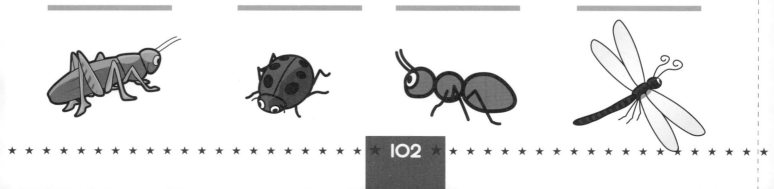

Color one box for each bug found in the picture.

1 2 3 4 5

Which bugs appears the most? Circle it.

The Penny

1 penny = 1 cent

This is the front of a penny.

This is the back of a penny.

If you have 2 pennies,
how many cents do you have?

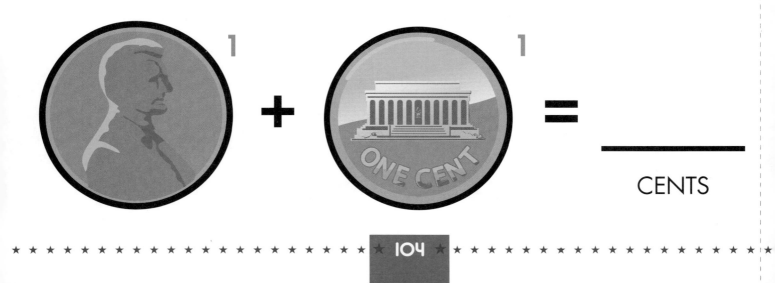

1 + 1 = ____

CENTS

The Nickel

1 nickel = 5 cents

This is the front of a nickel.

This is the back of a nickel.

If you have 1 nickel and 1 penny
how many cents do you have?

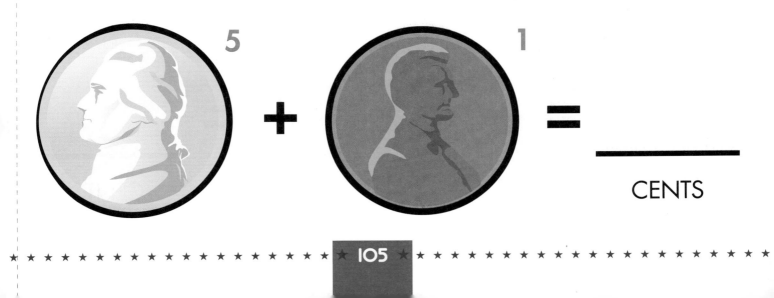

5 + 1 = _____

CENTS

The Dime

1 dime = 10 cents

This is the front of a dime.

This is the back of a dime.

If you have 1 nickel and 1 dime,
how many cents do you have?

 5 **+**  10 **=** _____

CENTS

The Quarter

1 quarter = 25 cents

This is the front of a quarter.

This is the back of a quarter.

If you have 1 quarter and 1 penny,
how many cents do you have?

25   +   1   = _____

CENTS

Numbers & Counting

Let's Learn How To Count Money

1 dime = 2 nickels

1 quarter = 2 dimes + 1 nickel

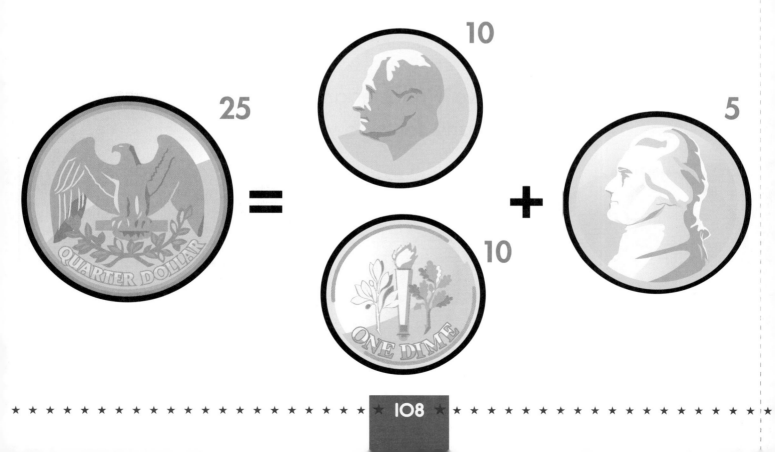

Count the Coins in the Piggy Bank

Count the number of coins in each piggy bank and write the answer in the boxes below.

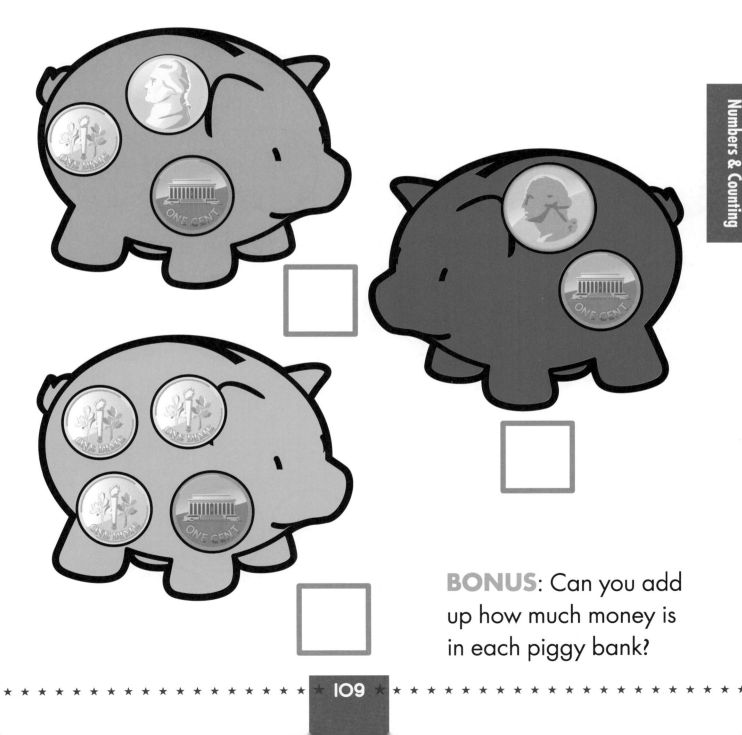

BONUS: Can you add up how much money is in each piggy bank?

Counting Money

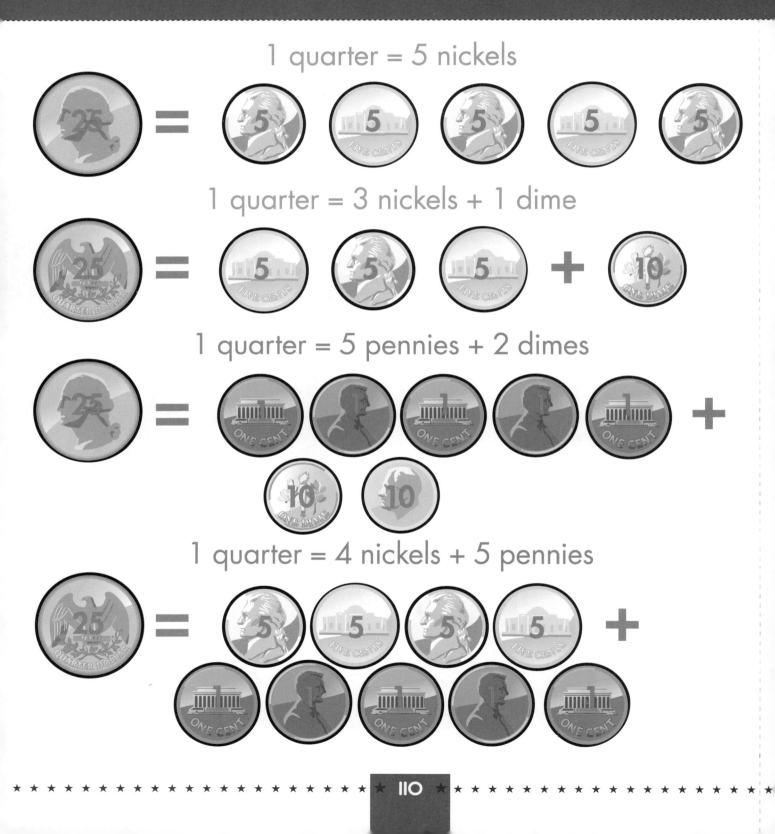

1 quarter = 5 nickels

1 quarter = 3 nickels + 1 dime

1 quarter = 5 pennies + 2 dimes

1 quarter = 4 nickels + 5 pennies

Addition

Count how many spots there are on the back of each ladybug and then write the number on the line. Add those two numbers together to find out how many spots in all.

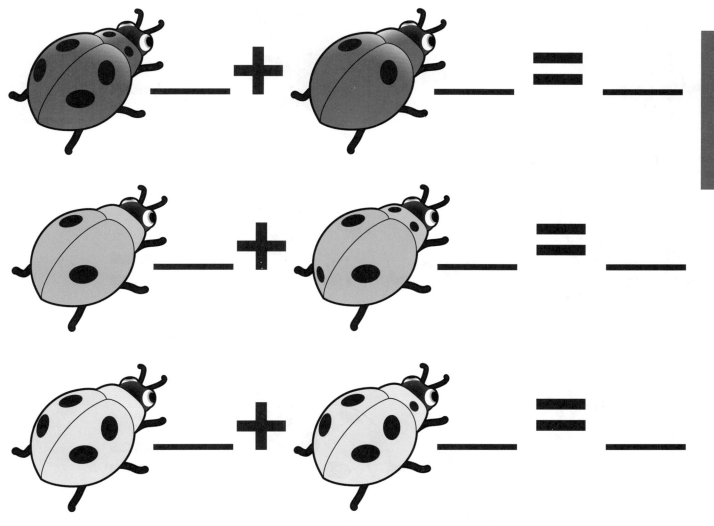

Subtraction

Count how many spots there on each ladybug and
write the number on the line. Then subtract the second number
from the first to get your answer.

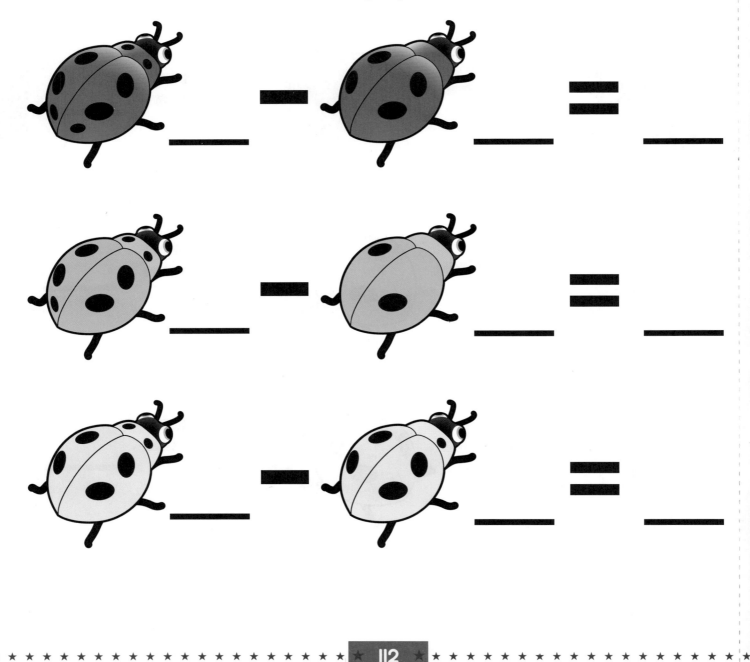

RED
ORANGE
YELLOW
GREEN
Colors
BLUE
PURPLE

★ 113 ★

The Color Red

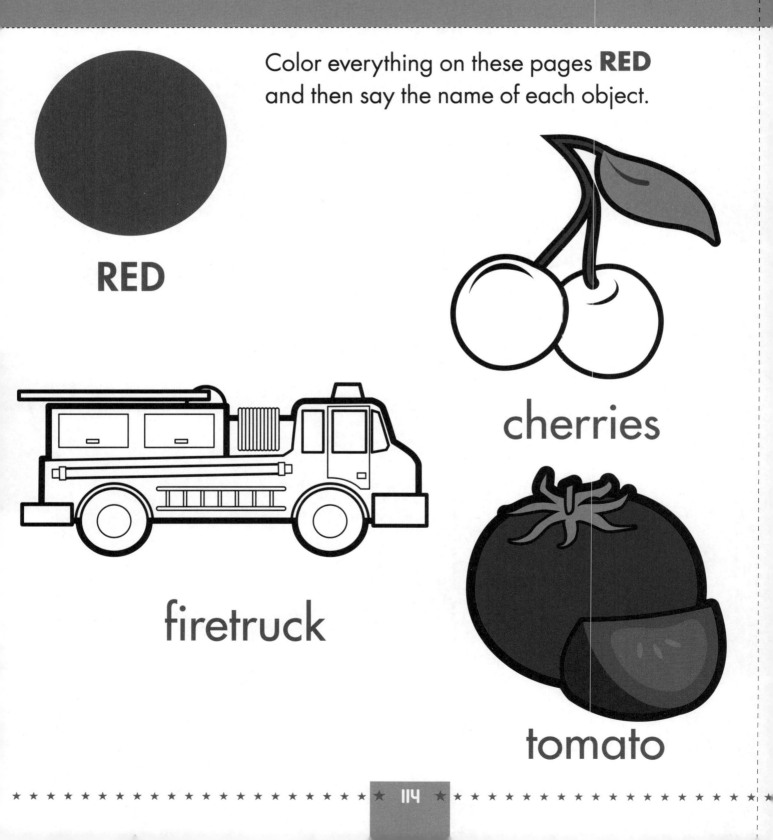

Color everything on these pages **RED** and then say the name of each object.

RED

cherries

firetruck

tomato

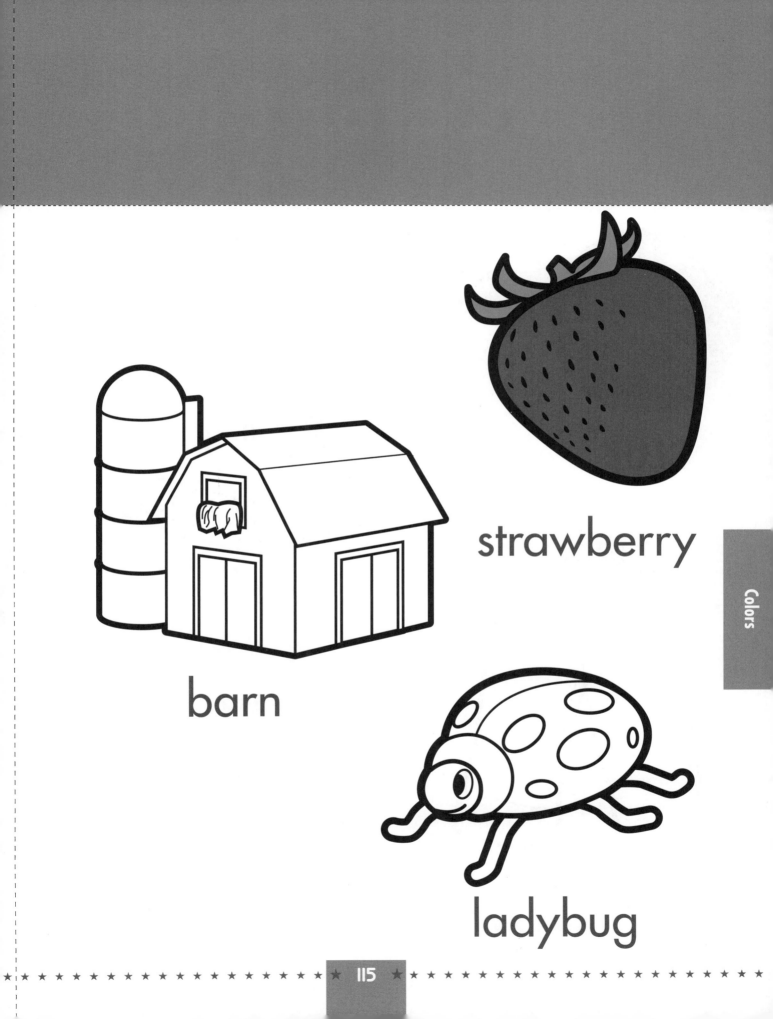

strawberry

barn

ladybug

The Color Blue

BLUE

Color everything on these pages **BLUE** and then say the name of each object.

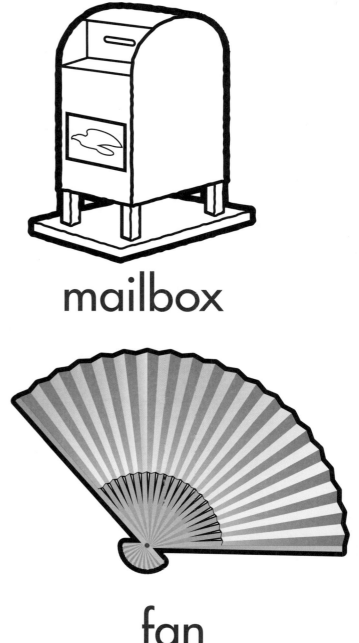

mailbox

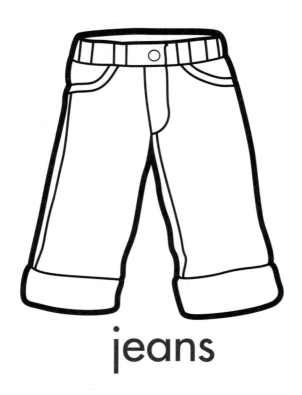

jeans

fan

whale

car

The Color Yellow

Color everything on these pages **YELLOW** and then say the name of each object.

YELLOW

sun

banana

bee

chick

cheese

corn

The Color Green

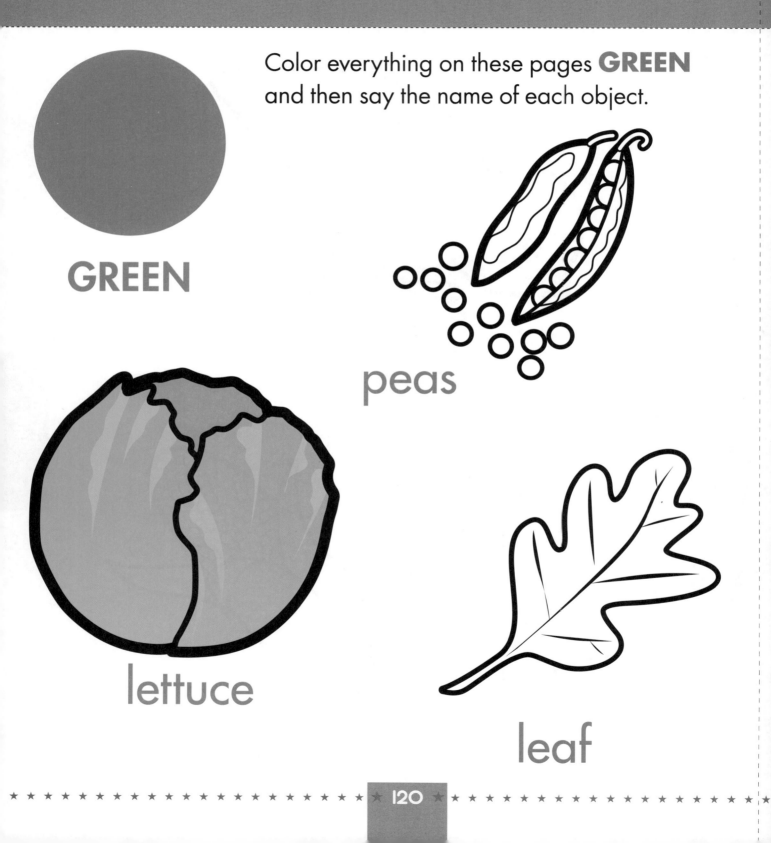

GREEN

Color everything on these pages **GREEN** and then say the name of each object.

peas

lettuce

leaf

alligator

frog

snake

The Color Orange

Color everything on these pages **ORANGE** and then say the name of each object.

ORANGE

carrot

orange

goldfish

pumpkin

lollipop

The Color Purple

PURPLE

Color everything on this page **PURPLE** then say the name of each object.

violets

crayon

grapes

The Color Brown

BROWN

Color everything on this page **BROWN** then say the name of each object.

bear

peanuts

guitar

The Color White

Everything on this page is WHITE.
Say the name of each object.

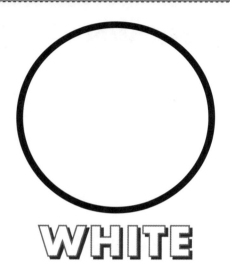

WHITE

cloud

duck

snowman

The Color Black

BLACK

Color everything on this page **BLACK** then say the name of each object.

cat

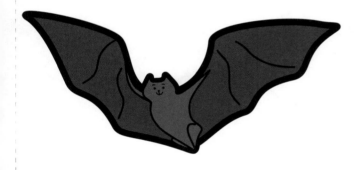

bat

ant

Yellow

Circle all of the foods that are **YELLOW**.

Red

Circle all of the foods that are **RED**.

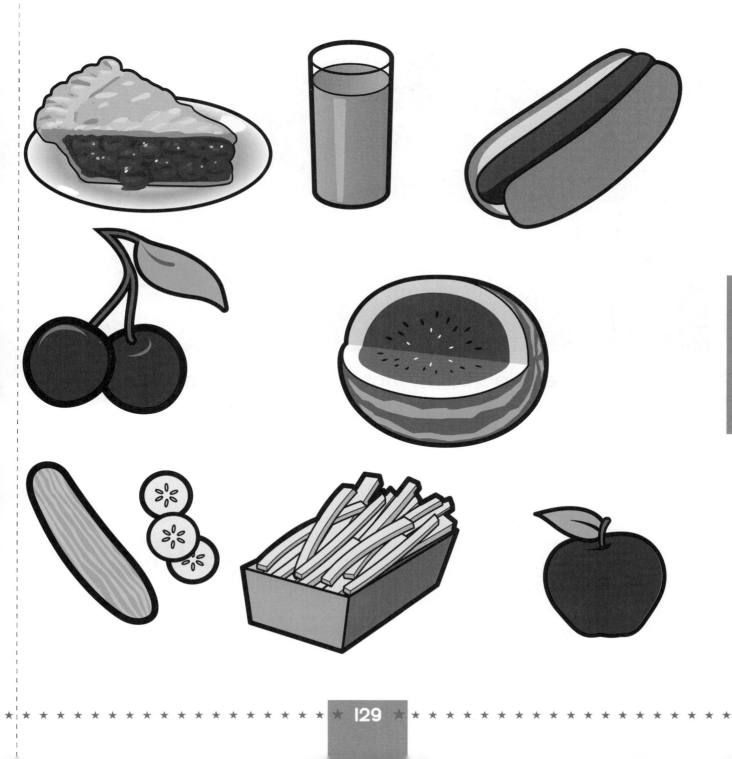

Colors

Rainbow

These are the colors in a rainbow.

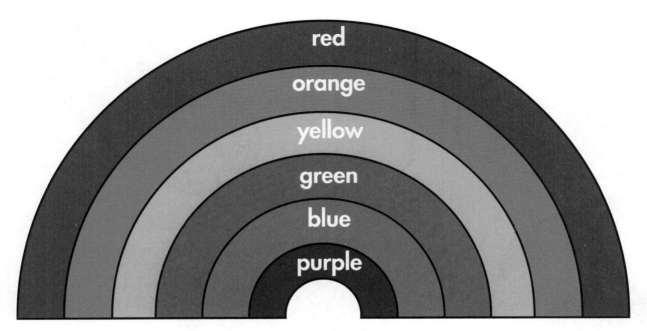

Circle the colors below that are not in the rainbow.

brown

yellow

orange

gray

pink

green

Matching Stars

Draw a line to match each color with its name.

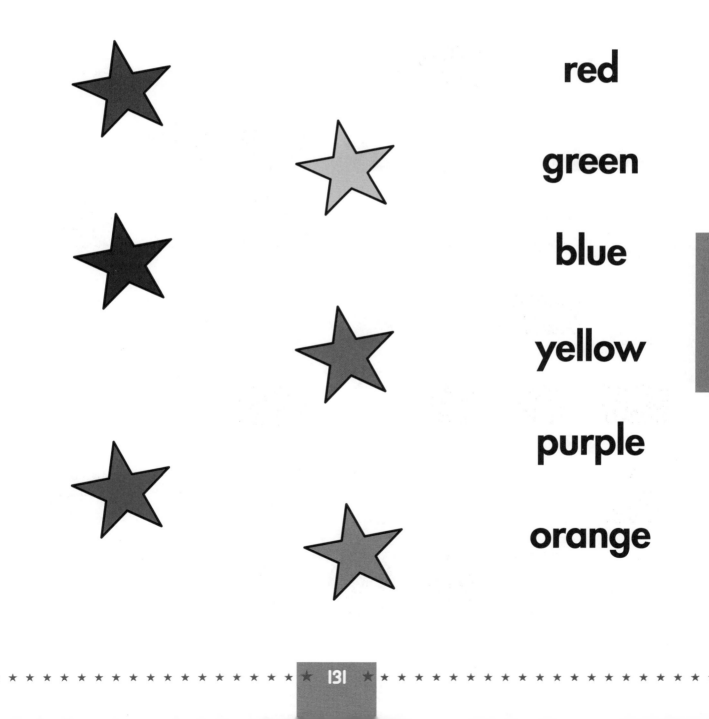

red

green

blue

yellow

purple

orange

Colors

Hungry Rabbit

Draw a line along the path that shows **ORANGE** circles and **GREEN** triangles to help the rabbit find the carrot.

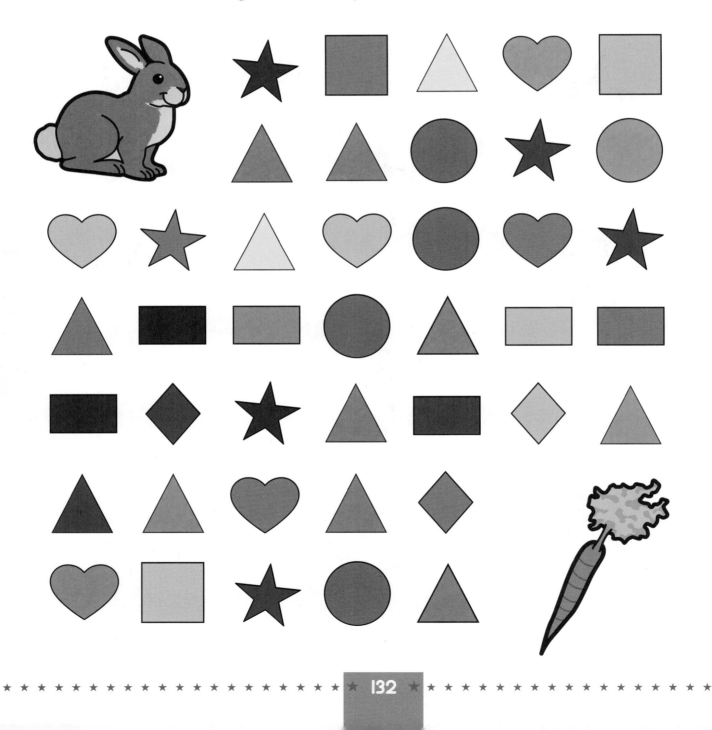

You Can Color

Let's get ready to paint. First, we need to add all the **COLORS** to the palette. Can you color them in?

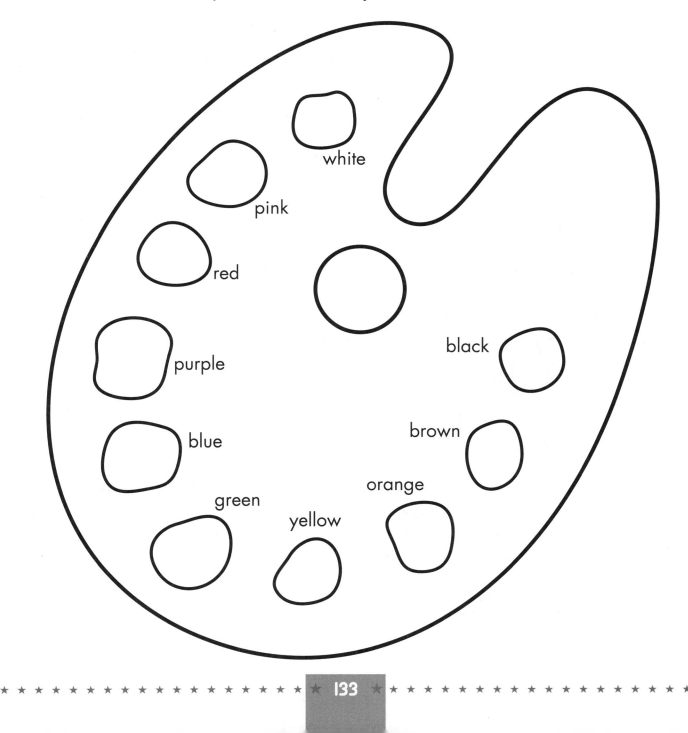

Colors

Circus Fun

Color the fun circus below.

Name the Color

Look at all of the colors and say each name out loud.

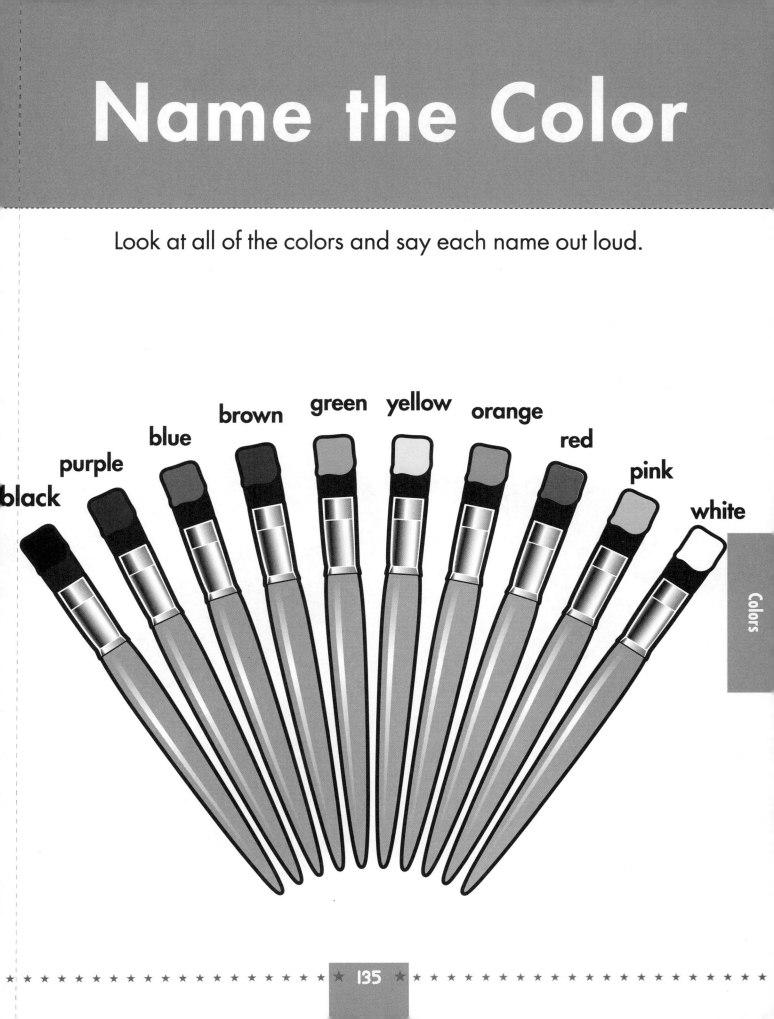

black purple blue brown green yellow orange red pink white

Colors

What Color?

black **purple** **blue** **brown** green yellow **orange** **red**

What color are the
objects on this page?
If you know, write the
answer in the box.

Farmyard Fun

Color the barn and farm animals.

Matching Hearts

Circle the heart that is the same as the first heart in each row.

Missing Colors

What colors are missing from the rainbow?
Can you color them in?

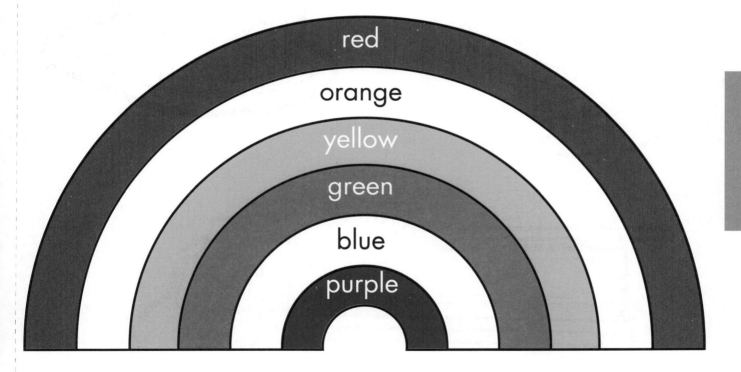

red

orange

yellow

green

blue

purple

Firefighting Fun

Get out your **RED** crayon--it's time to color!

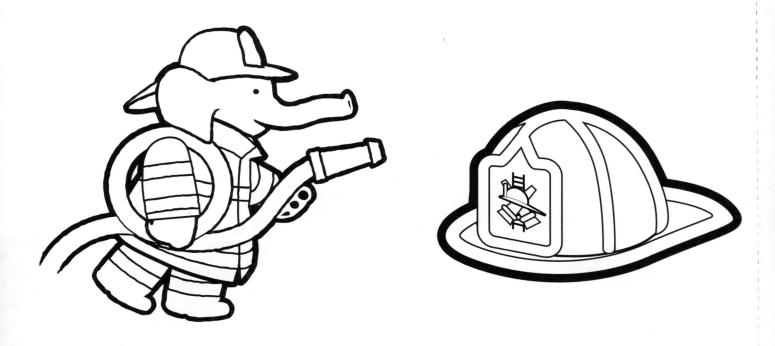

Wrong Color

Some of the objects below are the wrong color.
Circle the mistakes.

Colors

Find the Cheese

Draw a line along the path of **YELLOW** triangles and **BLUE** circles to lead the mouse to the cheese.

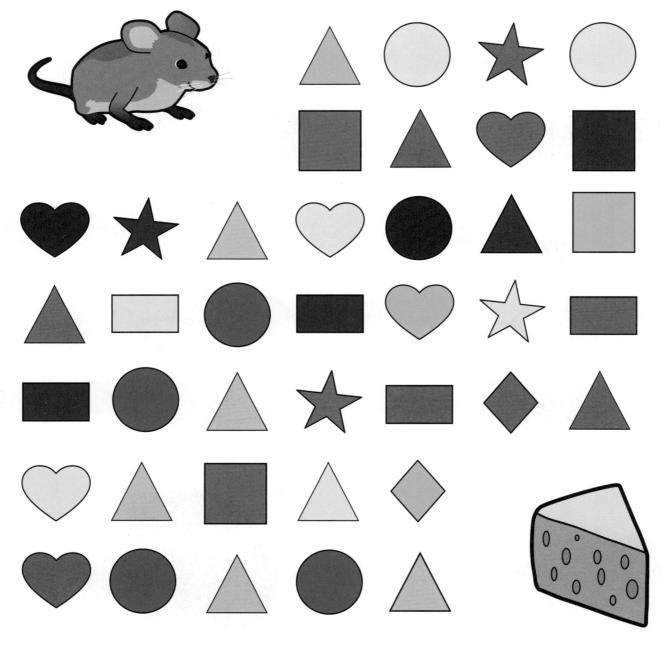

What Color?

black **purple** **blue** **brown** green yellow **orange** **red**

What color are the objects on this page? If you know, write the answer in the box.

What Color?

black **purple** **blue** **brown** green yellow **orange** **red**

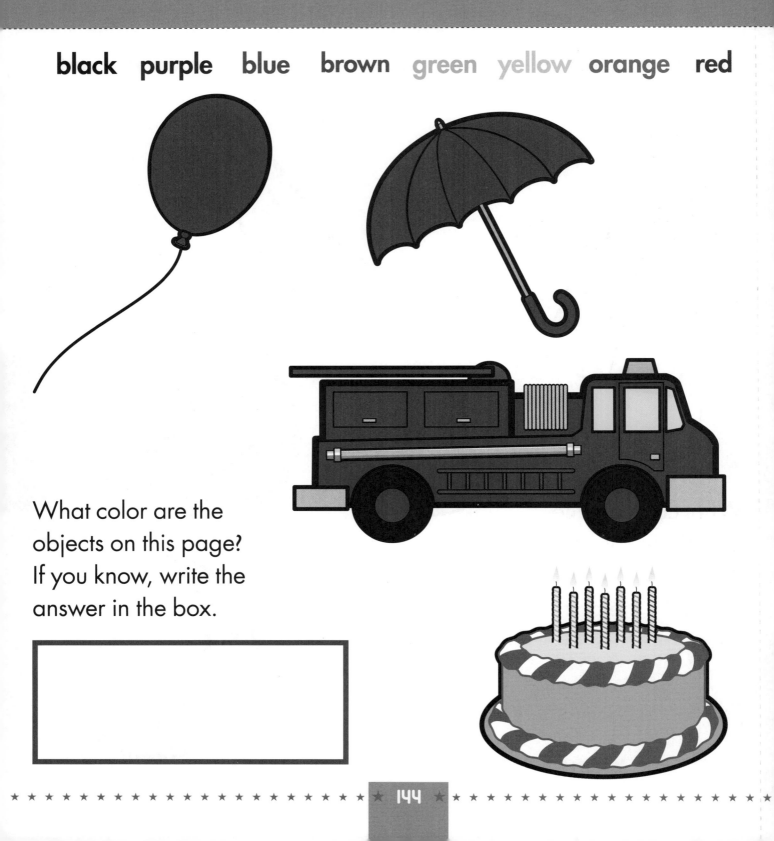

What color are the objects on this page? If you know, write the answer in the box.

Color Match

Draw a line between the two objects that are the same color.

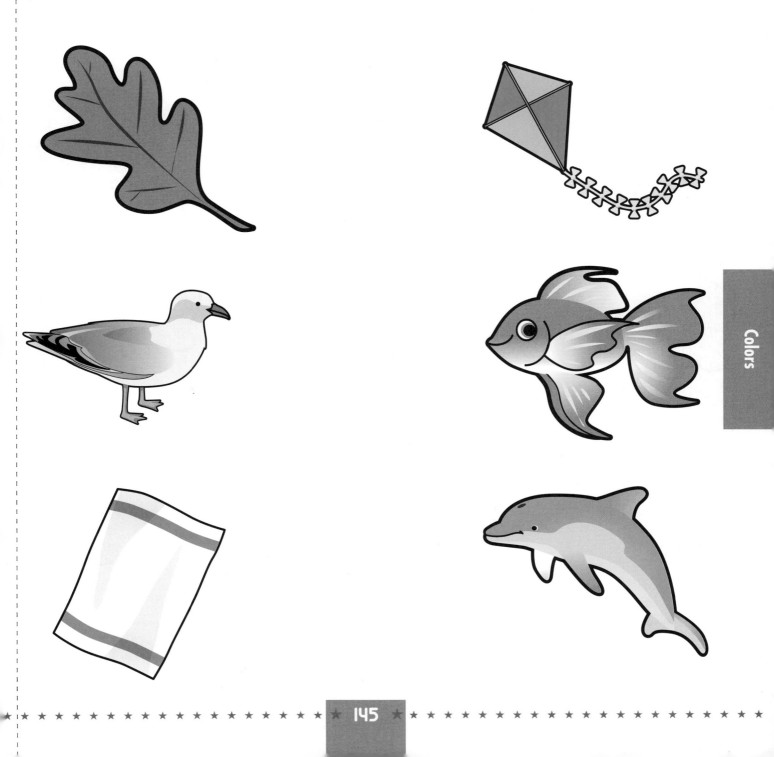

Colors

Color Graph

Fill in one space of the graph for each piggy bank in its color.
The space for the **BLUE** piggy banks have been filled in for you.

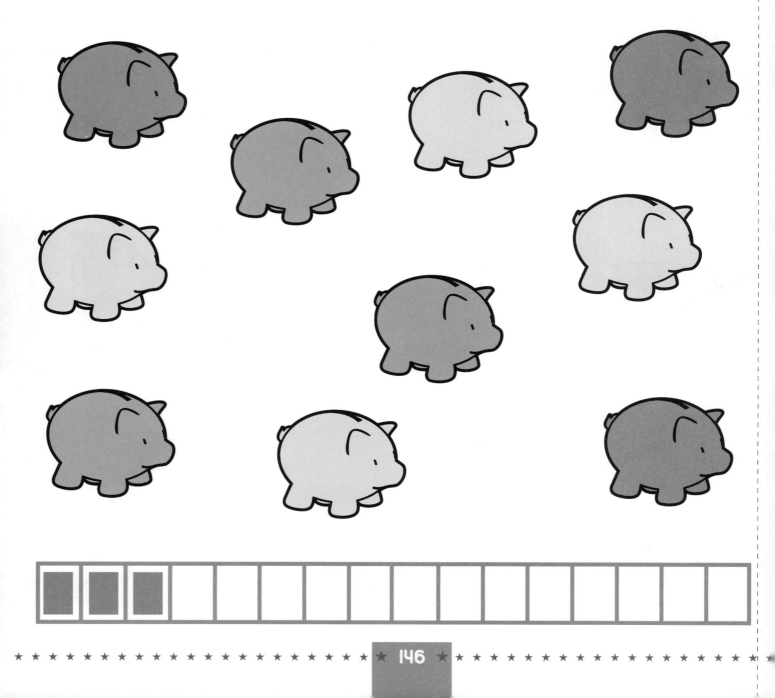

Orange

Circle all of the foods that are **ORANGE**.

Writing Colors

Now practice writing the names of the colors
by tracing the dotted lines of the letters.

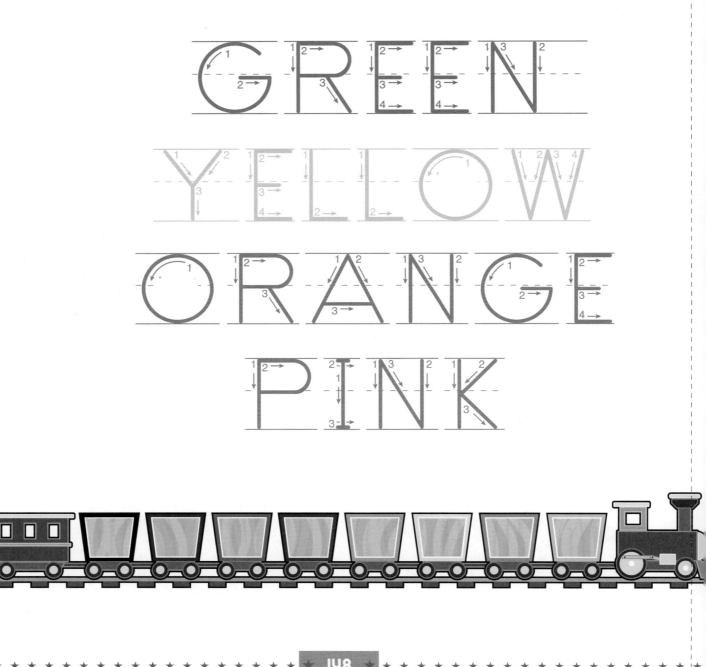

BROWN
PURPLE
BLACK
BLUE

What Color?

black   **purple**   **blue**   **brown**   green   yellow   **orange**   **red**

What color are the objects on this page? If you know, write the answer in the box.

SQUARE

CIRCLE

Shapes

OVAL

RECTANGLE

DIAMOND

Circle

Practice drawing **CIRCLES** by following the dotted lines.

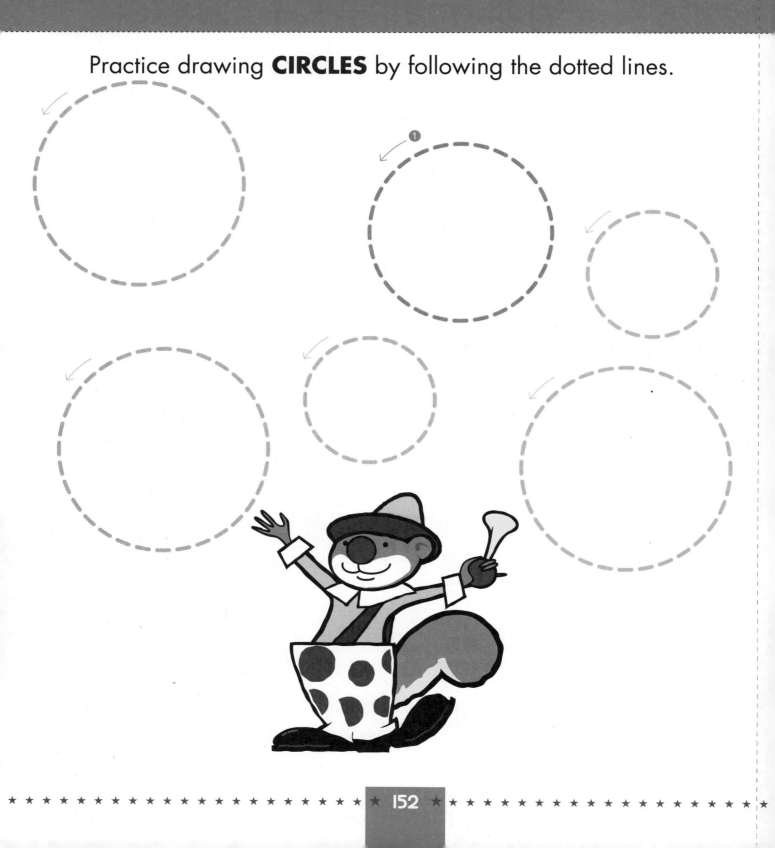

Square

Practice drawing **SQUARES** by following the dotted lines.

Triangle

Practice drawing **TRIANGLES** by following the dotted lines.

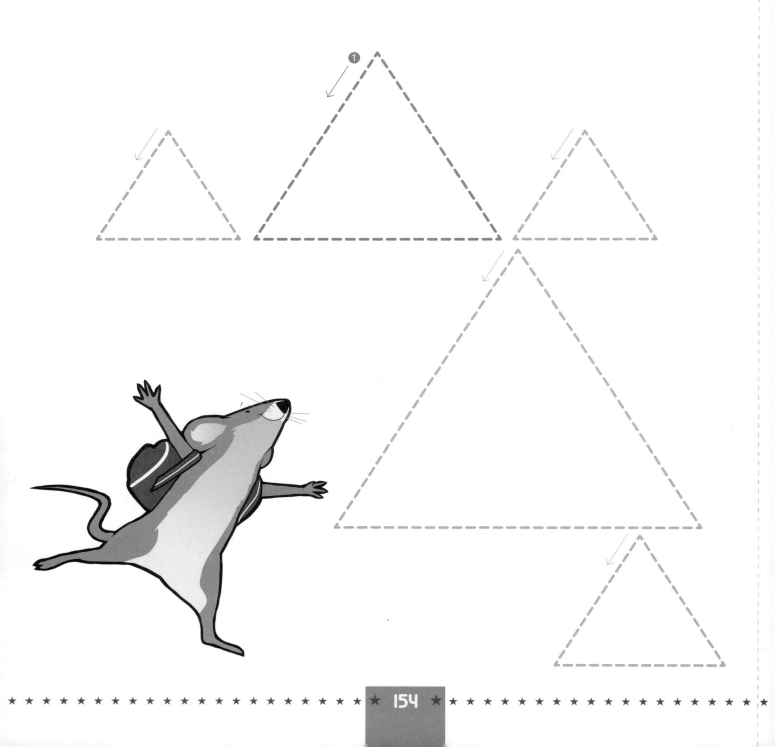

Rectangle

Practice drawing **RECTANGLES** by following the dotted lines.

Oval

Practice drawing **OVALS** by following the dotted lines.

Color the Shapes

Color only the **CIRCLES** on this page in **red**.

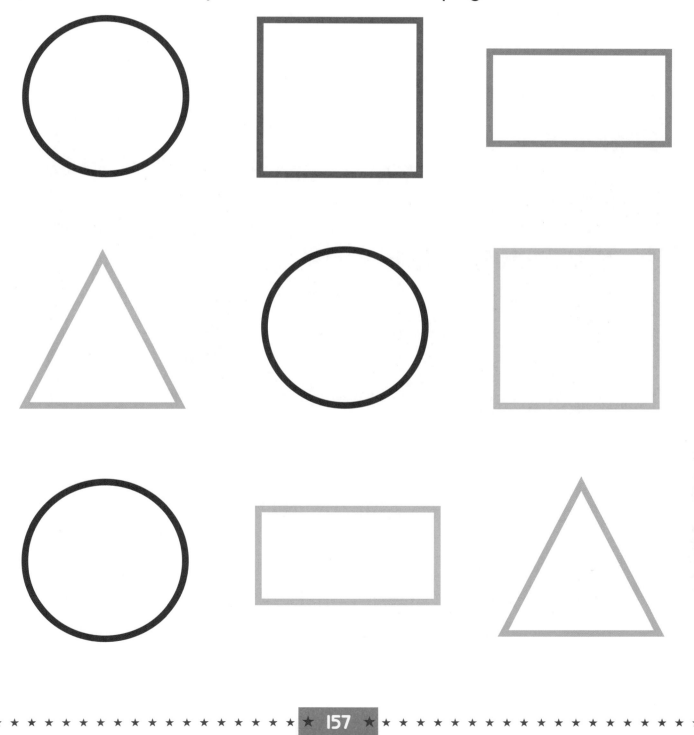

Shapes

Find the Shapes

Welcome to the circus of shapes!
See how many circles, squares, hearts, stars,
rectangles, ovals, and triangles you can find.

Shapes

Rectangle

Color the three **RECTANGLES** on this page.

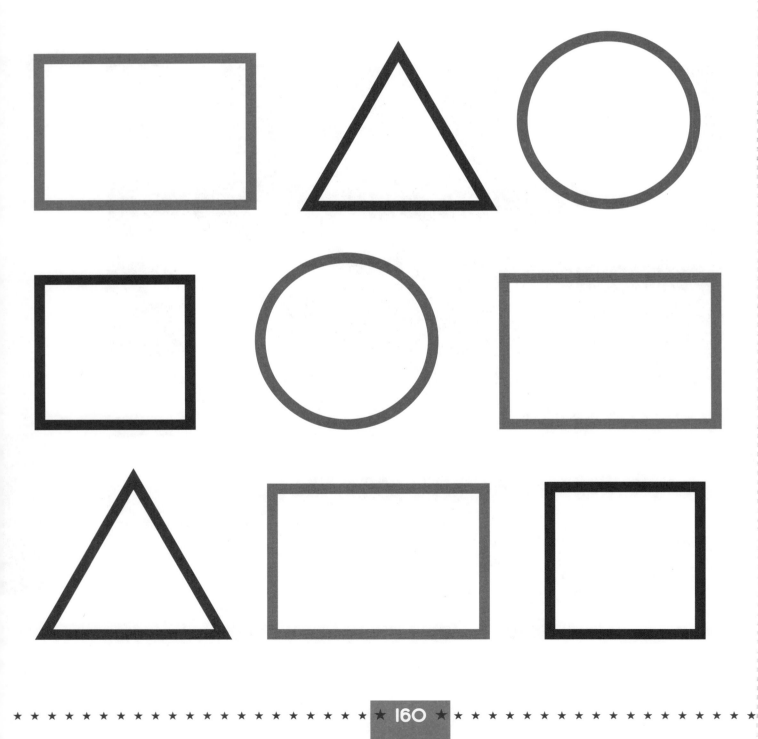

Triangle

Color the three **TRIANGLES** on this page.

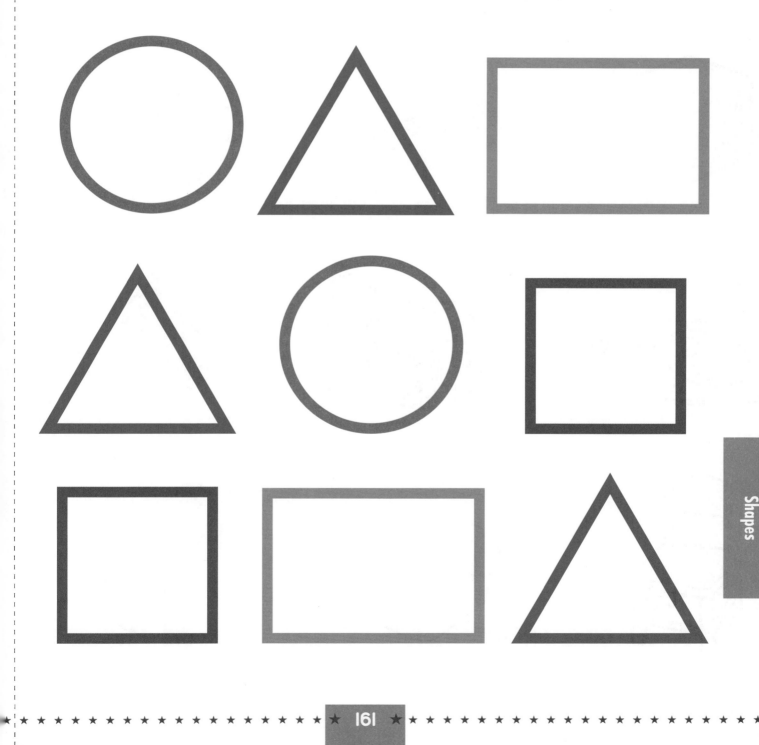

Find the

Find and circle all of the **SQUARES** on this page.

Find the

Find and circle all of the **TRIANGLES** on this page.

Shapes

Match the Shapes

Draw lines to match the shapes to the toys.

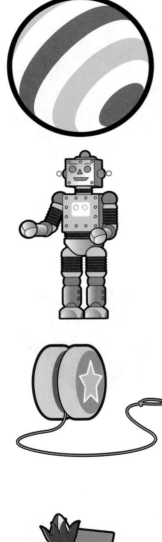

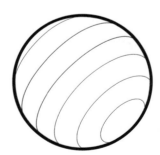

Complete the Pattern

Look at the patterns below.
See if you can figure out what shape comes next.
Draw the shape at the end of the row.

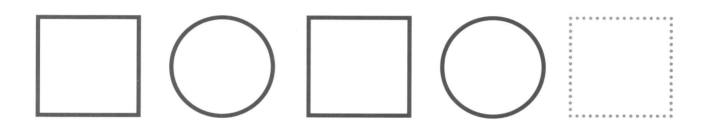

Shapes

Connect the Dots

Begin with number 1 and connect the dots to see the shape.
Color it in when you are done.

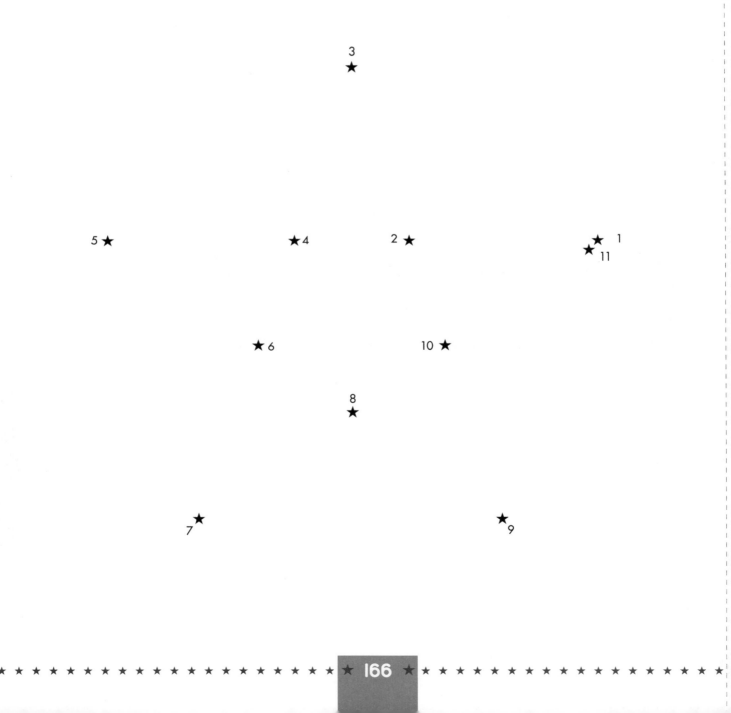

Shapes at the Beach

Find a circle, square, triangle, rectangle, oval, and star in the picture of the beach.

Shapes in Town

Find and trace all of the shapes in the town below.

Find the

Find and circle all of the **CIRCLES** on this page.

Find the

Find and circle all of the **RECTANGLES** on this page.

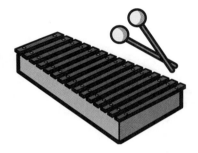

Shapes

Carefully look at the different shapes below.
Circle the triangles with a **RED** crayon, the circles with a **BLUE** crayon, and the squares with a **GREEN** crayon.

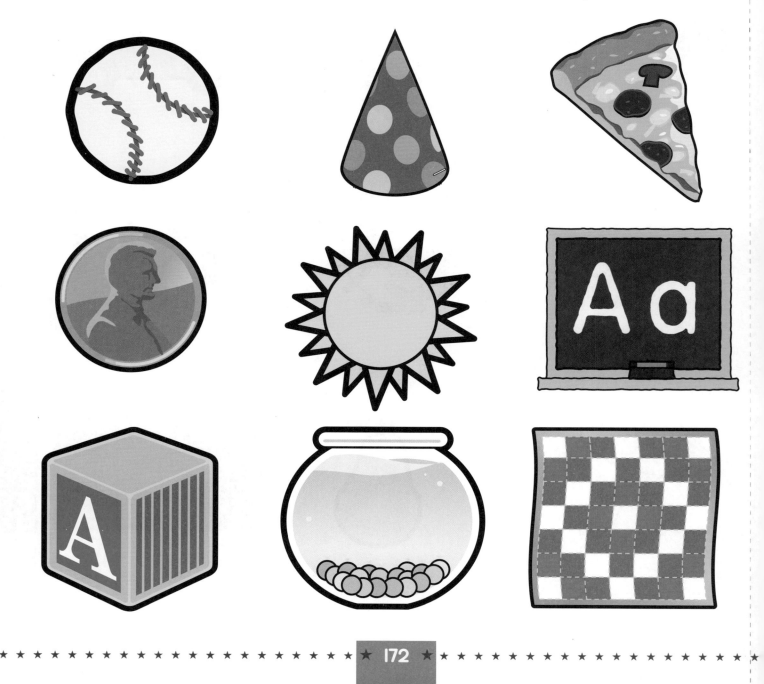

BIG BIGGER

Sizes, Comparisons, & Opposites

BIGGEST

Same Size

Look at the pictures in each box.
Circle the pictures that are the **SAME** size.

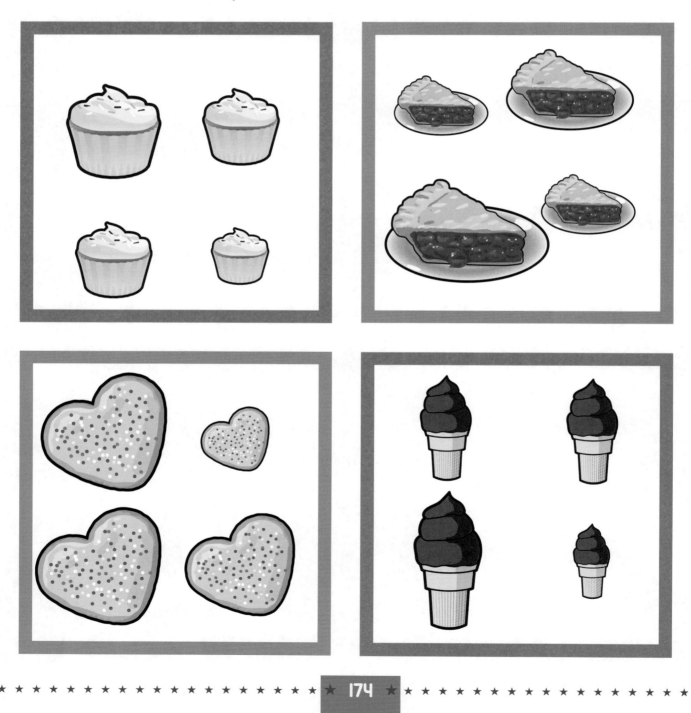

Big and Bigger

Look at the pictures below.
In each row, circle the picture that is **BIGGER** than the others.

Which is Different?

Look at these pairs carefully.
Circle the pairs that don't quite match.

Matching Mice

Each mouse has another mouse that is exactly like it, except for one. Can you circle the mouse that does not have a match?

Big and Little

A tiger  is **BIG**.

A kitten  is **little**.

Circle the animals below that are **little**.

Find the Difference

Two of these presents are **different** from the rest.
Circle the two that are **different**.

Sizes, Comparisons, & Opposites

Same and Different

Circle one object in each row that is different from the others.

What is Different?

There are 4 differences between the pictures of the farmers.
Can you find and circle them all?

Sizes, Comparisons, & Opposites

Top and Bottom

The kids are climbing all over the playground. Circle the ones at the **top** of the slides. Now cross out the ones at the **bottom**.

Near and Far

Circle the kid playing football who is **far** away.
Now cross out the one that is **near**.

Which kid is in front of the tree?
Which kid is behind the tree?

Above and Below

Circle the kid that is **above** the monkey bars.
Cross out the one that is **below**.

Which kid is going up on the see-saw?
Which kid is going down?

Find the Differences

Look carefully at the pictures below.
Can you find and circle the 3 differences?

Opposites

Look carefully at the pictures below.
What is the opposite of **CLEAN**? What is the opposite of **SHORT**?
Complete the words that are **OPPOSITES**.

CLEAN   **DIRTY**

SHORT

LONG

Opposites

Look carefully at the pictures below.
What is the opposite of **DAY**? What is the opposite of **FRONT**?
Complete the words that are **OPPOSITES**.

DAY

NIGHT

FRONT

BACK

Opposites

Look carefully at the pictures and draw a line connecting each word to its opposite.

fat

fast

slow

strong

weak

thin

Opposites

Look carefully at the pictures and draw a line connecting each word to its opposite.

happy

cold

open

sad

hot

closed

Tall

How **tall** are you?
Draw a picture below of something **taller** than you.

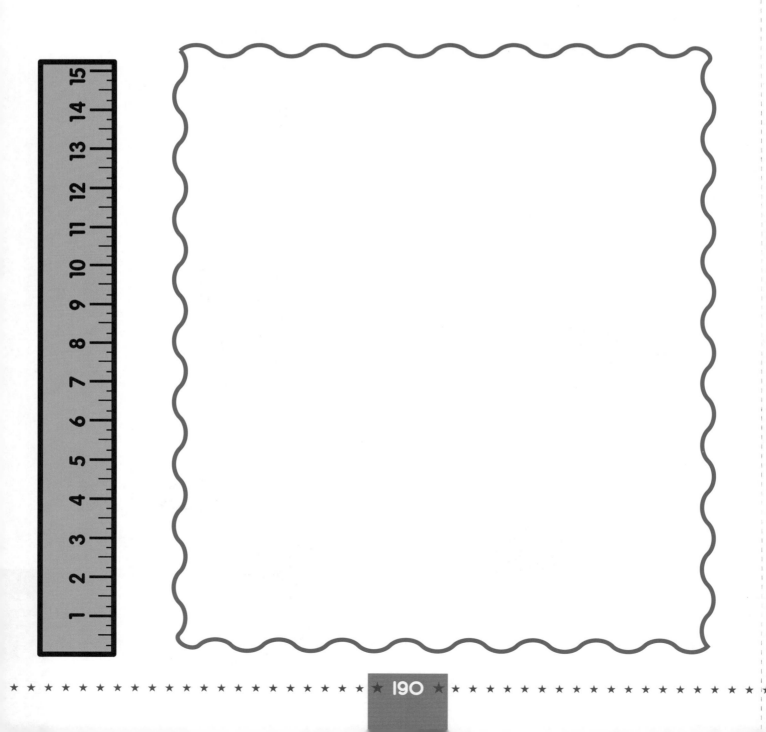

Short

Draw a picture below of something **shorter** than you.

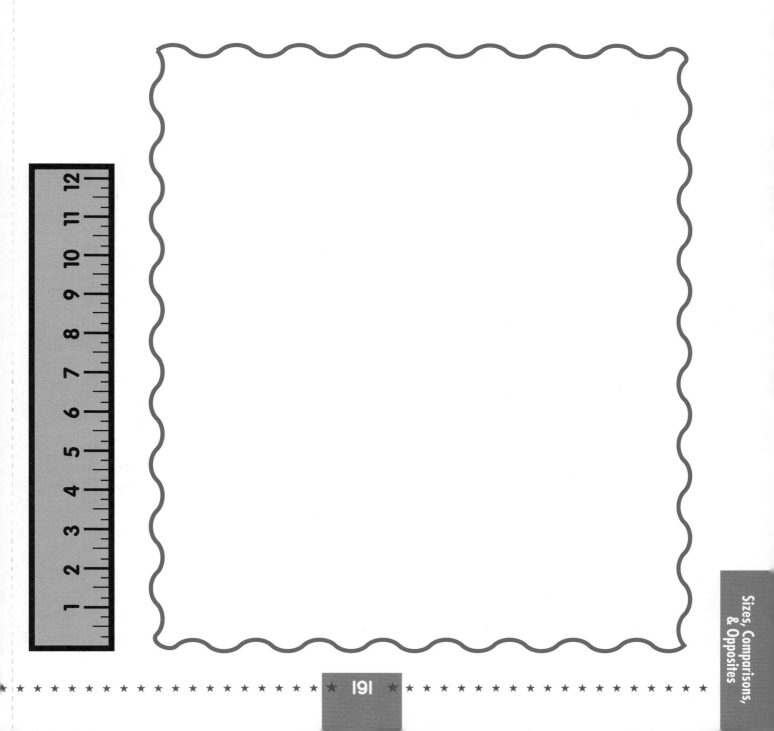

Opposites

Look carefully at the pictures below.
What is the opposite of **EMPTY**? What is the opposite of **ASLEEP**?
Complete the words and then color in the pictures.

EMPTY   FULL

ASLEEP   AWAKE

Opposites

Look carefully at the pictures below.
What is the opposite of **SAD**? What is the opposite of **CLOSED**?
Complete the words that are **OPPOSITES**

SAD

HAPPY

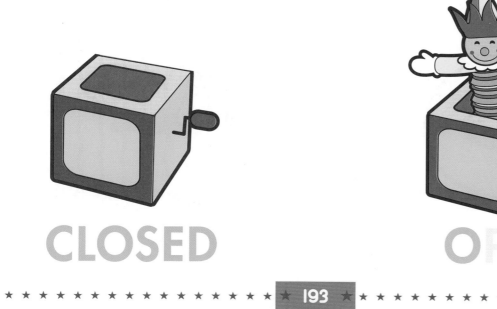

CLOSED

OPEN

Opposites

Look carefully at the pictures below.
What is the opposite of **LITTLE**? What is the opposite of **WET**?
Complete the words that are **OPPOSITES**.

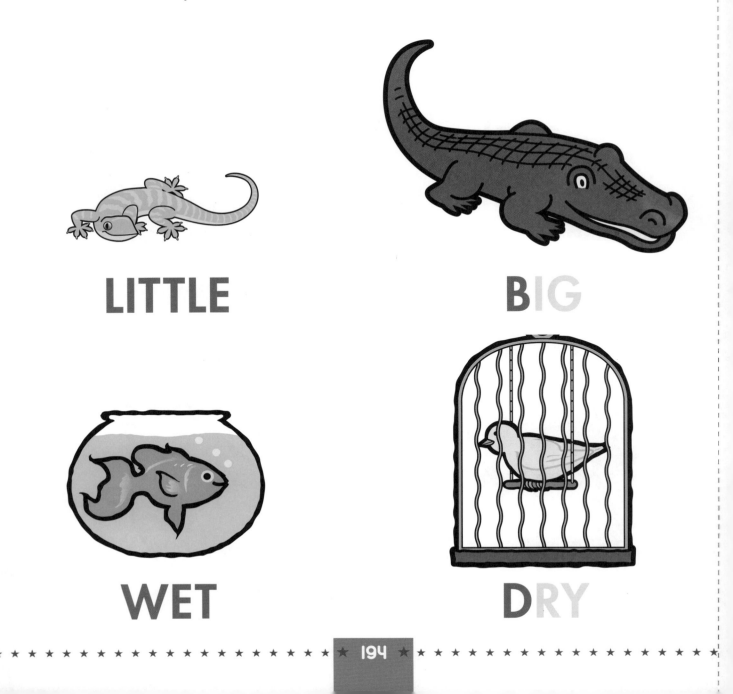

LITTLE

BIG

WET

DRY

WHAT GOES

Combinations

TOGETHER?

What Goes Together?

Circle the two pictures in each row that belong together.

Combinations

Circle the two pictures in each row that belong together.

What Goes Together?

Circle the two animals in each row that belong together.

Combinations

Circle the two animals in each row that belong together.

Does Not Belong

Circle the picture in each row that does NOT belong.

What is a Part of Your Food?

Draw a line from the ingredient to the food it makes.

Connect the Objects

Draw a line between the people and their objects.

Combinations

Draw something else that can go with each group.

Combinations

Draw something else that can go with each group.

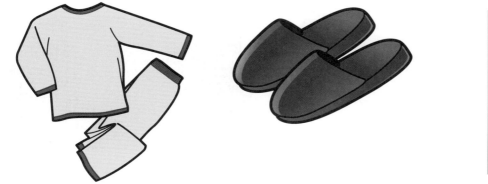

Combinations

Circle the two pictures in each row that belong together.

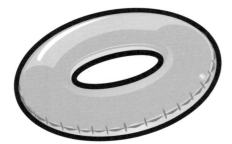  

  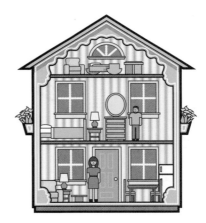

 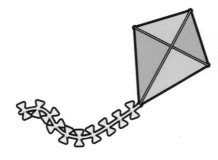 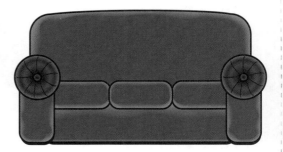

MY SISTER

MY DAD

Our World

MY MOM

ME

Rooms in a House

Draw a line from the room to its name.

BEDROOM

BATHROOM

KITCHEN

LIVING ROOM

Where do they go? Say the name of each thing below
and point to the room in the house where it belongs.

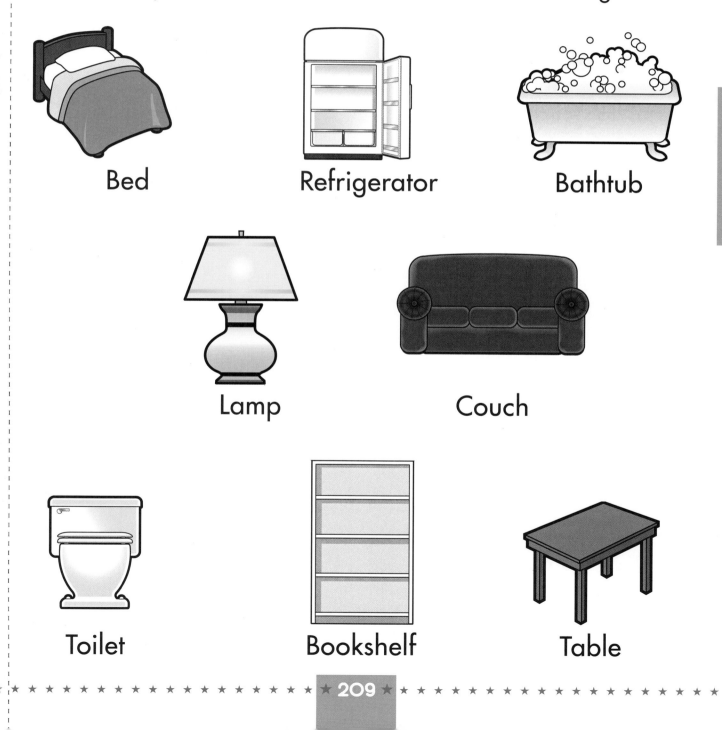

Bed

Refrigerator

Bathtub

Lamp

Couch

Toilet

Bookshelf

Table

My Room

Draw a picture of your room. Make sure to include your favorite toys!

Phone/Town

What is your **phone number**? Write it below.

(_ _ _) _ _ _ - _ _ _ _

What is the name of your **town**? Write it below.

_ _ _ _ _ _ _ _ _ _ _ _ _ _ _

What do you like to eat?

Circle the foods you like to eat.

My Family

Write the number of people in your family.

___ mother

___ father

___ sister

___ brother

___ grandmother

___ grandfather

___ uncle

___ aunt

___ cousins

Pets

Do you have a **pet**? If so, circle it below.
If not, circle one you'd like to have.

The Five Senses: Touch

Circle the items below that feel soft to the **touch**.

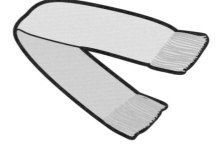

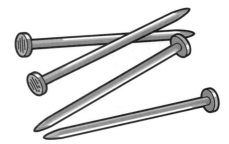

The Five Senses: Taste

Connect the dots, beginning with number 1, to reveal a sweet treat. Color it your favorite flavor.

1
2

3   4   7   8

5   6

The Five Senses: Smell

Circle the things below that **smell** good.

The Five Senses: Hearing

Color the things that make music.

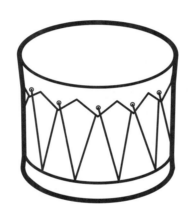

The Five Senses: See

Something silly is happening at the zoo! See if you can find and circle the 3 objects that don't belong.

Morning

Circle the picture below that happens **first** in the morning.

Putting on Shoes

Circle the picture that happened **before** Claire put on her shoes.

Ready for Bed

Look at the pictures below.
Write 1, 2, 3 and 4 to put them in order.

People in the Neighborhood

Can you name the jobs of everyone on this page?
Draw a line to match the people to their object.

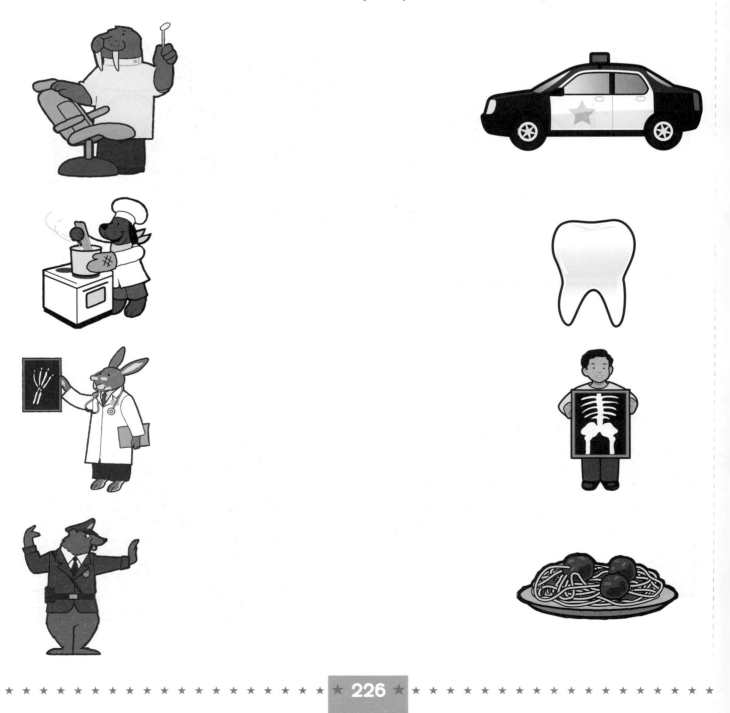

Draw a line between the people and where they work.

Picnic

Lila the hippo is having a picnic in the park.

Circle what she could bring for her picnic.

Signs

Find and circle the following directions in the puzzle below:
LEFT, **RIGHT**, **STOP**, **GO**, **YIELD**, **NEAR**, **FAR**

```
G  Y  A  P  S  E  U  T
R  A  B  N  V  E  G  O
I  U  P  E  A  Y  L  X
G  T  D  A  E  I  O  W
H  R  F  R  I  E  A  U
T  A  Y  F  T  L  R  N
U  L  D  L  Q  D  I  D
F  A  R  L  R  N  C  E
D  A  F  N  Q  D  A  R
A  Y  A  P  L  E  F  T
S  T  O  P  M  W  W  B
```

On the Road

Color what travels on the road.

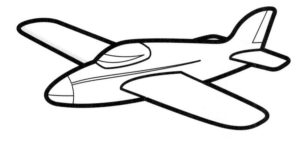

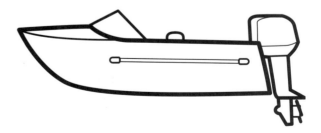

Telling Time

On a clock, the big hand shows the minutes. The little hand to shows the hour. In the picture below, the hour hand is pointing to the 3. The minute hand is pointing to the 12 (or 0 minutes). It is 3:00, or three o'clock.

In this picture, the hour hand is between numbers 1 and 2, and the minute hand is pointing to the number 30, so it is 1:30, or one thirty.

Telling Time

Each of the four clocks is telling you a different time.
Write down what time it is under each clock.

___ : ___ ___

___ : ___ ___

___ : ___ ___

___ : ___ ___

Telling Time

Each of the four clocks is telling you a different time.
Write down what time it is under each clock.

____ : ____ ____   ____ : ____ ____

____ : ____ ____   ____ : ____ ____

What to Wear?

Circle the clothes you wear to the **beach**.

What to Wear?

Circle the clothes you wear in the **snow**.

Washing Hands

There are germs on your hands. You are so small you can't see them. Germs can make you sick. If you wash your hands, it kills the germs. Can you color in the germs?

Washing Hands

Put the following steps for **washing hands** in the correct order by putting 1 to 5 in the box.

1. Wet hands   2. Use soap   **3. Lather, rub, and count to 20**
4. Rinse   **5. Dry off hands with a towel**

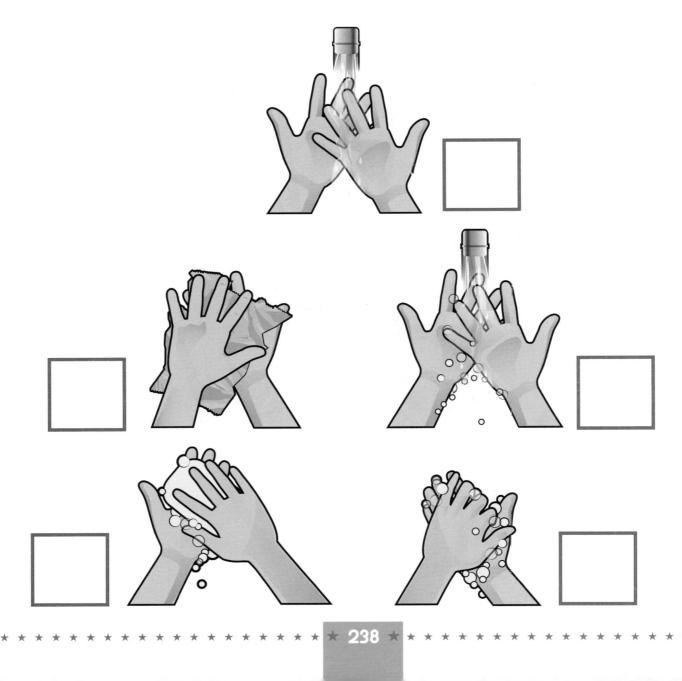

Your Teeth

How many teeth do I have?

I have _____ upper teeth.

I have _____ lower teeth.

I have _____ teeth altogether.

When do I brush my teeth?

I brush my teeth in the _____ and at _____.

After I brush, I _____ my teeth.

floss count

I eat healthy foods that are good for my teeth.

I like to eat: _____

I go to the _____ every six months to make
sure I don't have any cavities.

Brushing Teeth

Brush your teeth every morning and night
to keep them healthy and clean.
Put a number 1-5 in each box to show the
correct order in brushing your teeth.

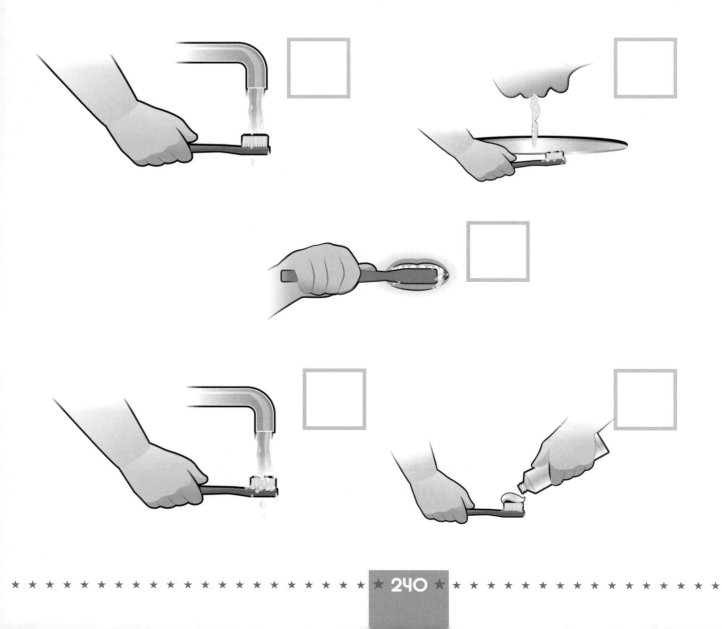

Seatbelts

Whenever you ride in a car, you must wear your **seatbelt**. Color the picture below of the panda buckled up for safety.

Helmets

Helmets are important for safety. Draw a line from the boy with the **helmet** to activities where he must wear a **helmet**.

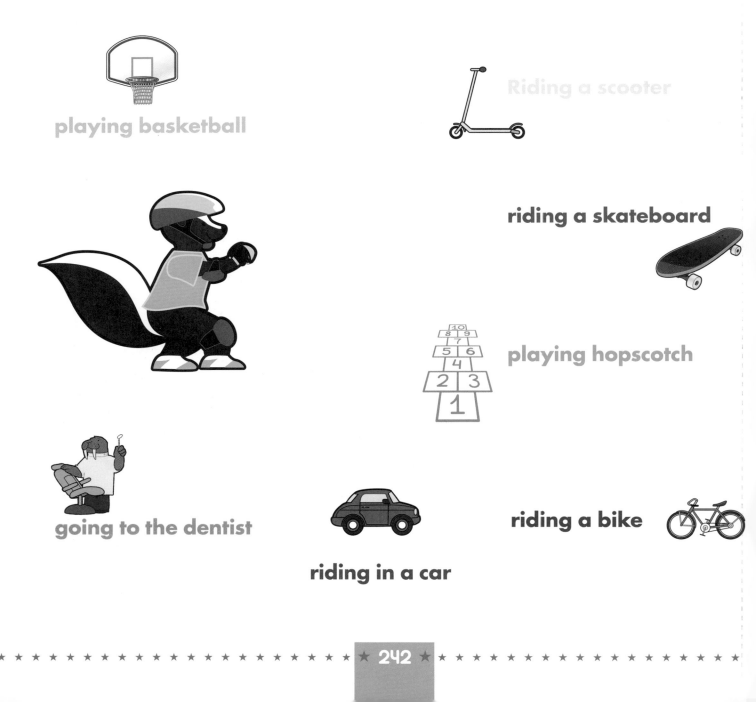

playing basketball

Riding a scooter

riding a skateboard

playing hopscotch

going to the dentist

riding in a car

riding a bike

Tying Your Shoe

Bunny Ears Method

Step 1 & 2 First make a knot for the bunny's head.
Take the laces and cross them over to make an "X".
Then, pull one lace through the bottom of the "X" and pull tight.

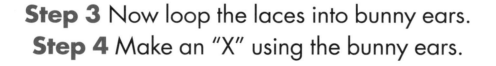

1

2

Step 3 Now loop the laces into bunny ears.
Step 4 Make an "X" using the bunny ears.

3

4

Step 5 Slide one ear under the "X."
Step 6 Pull tightly.

5

6

Crossing the Street

Before you cross a street, **Stop, Look, and Listen!**

Draw a line from each word to its matching picture.

STOP

LOOK

LISTEN

Draw a line between the traffic light color and what it means.

GO

STOP

SLOW

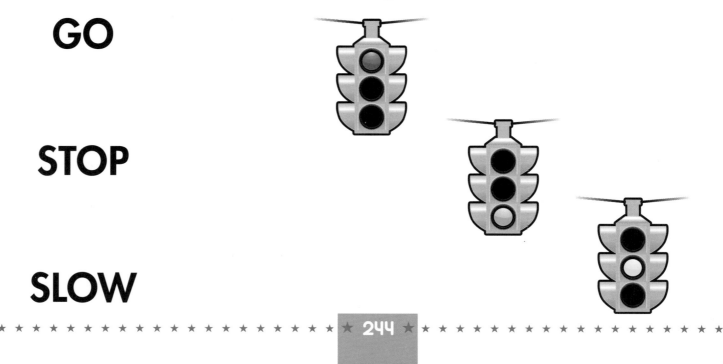

Nature & Science

PLANT IT

WATER IT

PICK IT

Weather

Draw a line connecting the **weather** to its name.

Sun

Rain

Wind

Snow

Rainy Day Gear

Circle the things you use to keep **dry**.

The Four Seasons: Winter

Winter occurs in four months:
December January **February March**
Below is a farm in **winter**.

Circle the words that describe the weather in **winter**.

Sunny Rainy Windy Snowy
Hot Cold Cool

Winter Fun

Circle what you can find outside when it is **winter**.

The Four Seasons: Spring

Spring occurs in four months:
March April May June
Below is a farm in **spring**.

Circle the words that describe the weather in **spring**.

Sunny Rainy Windy Snowy
Hot Cold Cool

Plants Grow

In **spring**, plants begin to grow. This picture shows the roots, leavwa, and flower of a plant. Can you find the roots? Circle them.

The Four Seasons: Summer

Summer occurs in four months:
June July **August** **September**
Below is a farm in **summer**.

Circle the words that describe the weather in **summer**.

Sunny Rainy Windy Snowy
Hot Cold Cool

Animals on a Farm

Color the animals below that live on a **farm**.

The Four Seasons: Fall

Fall occurs in four months:
September October November December
Below is a farm in **fall**.

Circle the words that describe the weather in **fall**.

Sunny Rainy Windy Snowy
Hot Cold Cool

Corn Maze

Help the pig eat its way through the maze to its piglet.

The Life of a Butterfly

1. First, a butterfly is born out of an egg as a caterpillar. **2.** It spends most of its life eating leaves. **3.** When it gets big enough, it attaches to a twig and forms a chrysalis or a cocoon.

3.

2.

1.

4. It hatches out of the chrysalis into a beautiful butterfly! Color the butterfly below.

4.

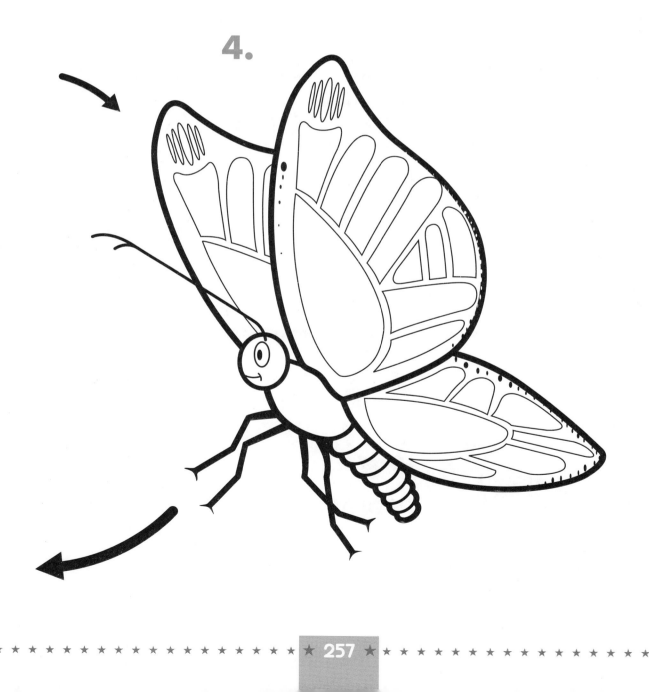

Find the Animals

Find and circle the animals in the puzzle shown below.
The first one has been done for you.

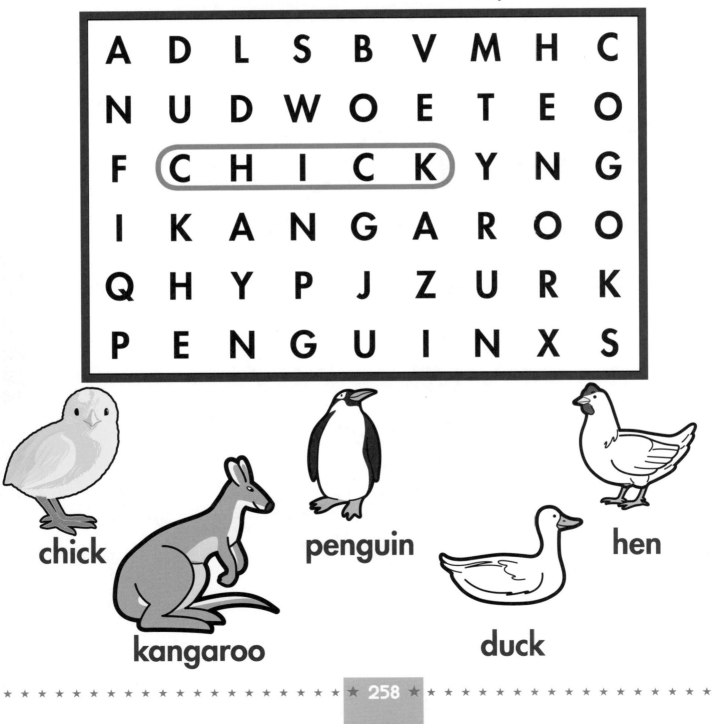

A	D	L	S	B	V	M	H	C
N	U	D	W	O	E	T	E	O
F	C	H	I	C	K	Y	N	G
I	K	A	N	G	A	R	O	O
Q	H	Y	P	J	Z	U	R	K
P	E	N	G	U	I	N	X	S

chick

kangaroo

penguin

duck

hen

Alive or Not?

Animals and plants are alive. Circle the objects that are **NOT** alive.

What Do They Make?

Each of the animals below provides something people need. Draw a line from each animal to the product we get from it.

Animals of the Ocean

All of these animals, except for one, live in or near the ocean.
Circle the animal that **DOES NOT** live in or near the sea.

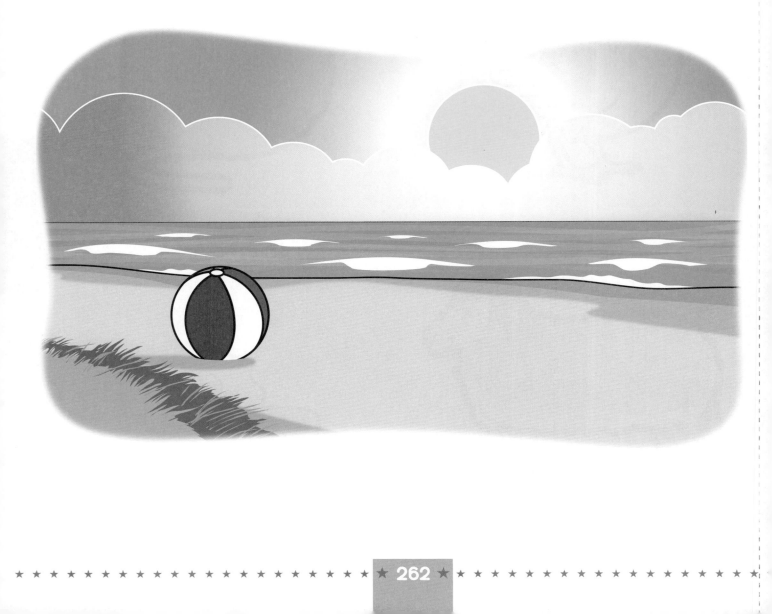

Animals of the Savanna

A **savanna** is a hot, dry grassland found in countries including Africa, Australia, and Madagascar.

All of these animals, except for one, live in the savanna. Circle the animal that **DOES NOT** live in the savanna.

Animals of the Forest

All of these animals, except for one, live in or near the **forest**.
Circle the animal that **DOES NOT** live in or near the **forest**.

Animals of a Pond or Lake

All of these animals, except for one, live in or near a **pond** or **lake**. Circle the animal that **DOES NOT** live in or near a **pond** or **lake**.

Where Do They Live?

Which of these animals live in the **forest**?

Which Ones Are Insects?

There are a lot of bugs on this page.
An **insect** is a bug with six or more legs.
Can you find and circle all of the insects on this page?

Color the Insects

Color the **insects** in the garden below.

Tree Climbers

The animals in the list below are all good **tree climbers**.
Find and circle the animals in the puzzle.
The words can be either across, up, or down.

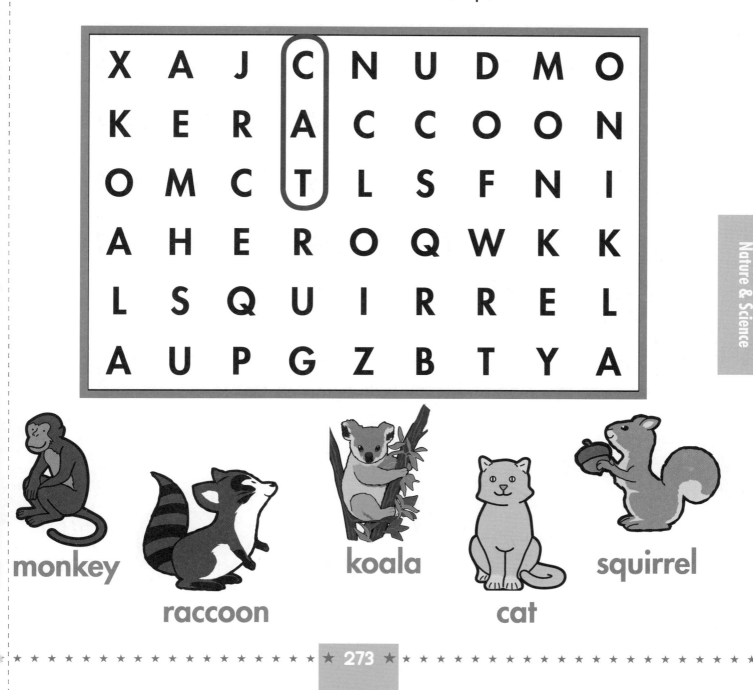

X	A	J	C	N	U	D	M	O
K	E	R	A	C	C	O	O	N
O	M	C	T	L	S	F	N	I
A	H	E	R	O	Q	W	K	K
L	S	Q	U	I	R	R	E	L
A	U	P	G	Z	B	T	Y	A

monkey

raccoon

koala

cat

squirrel

Animals with Hooves

The animals below all have **hooves**, which protect their feet.
Find and circle the animals in the puzzle.
The words can be either across, up, or down.

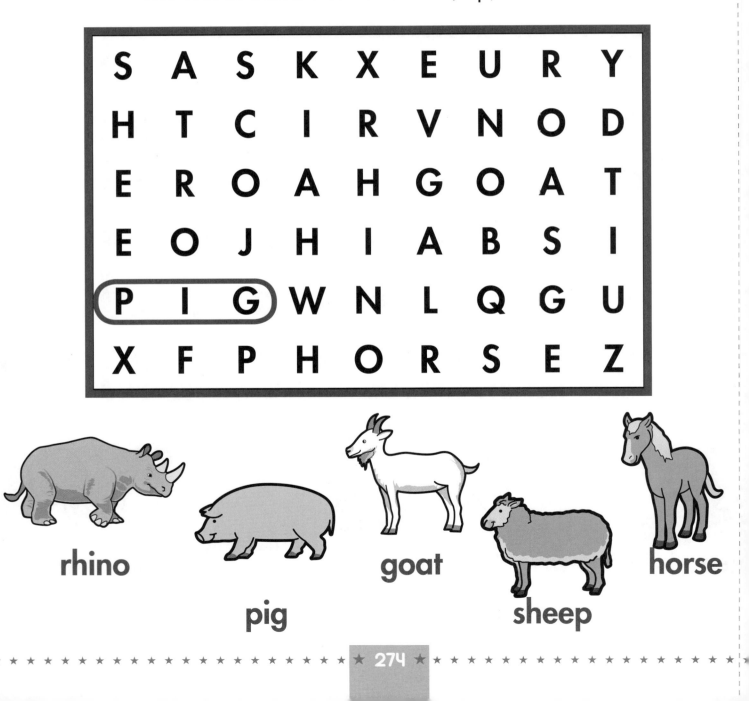

S	A	S	K	X	E	U	R	Y
H	T	C	I	R	V	N	O	D
E	R	O	A	H	G	O	A	T
E	O	J	H	I	A	B	S	I
P	I	G	W	N	L	Q	G	U
X	F	P	H	O	R	S	E	Z

rhino

pig

goat

sheep

horse

Baby Animals on the Farm

All of these baby animals live on a farm except for **one**.
Circle the one that **DOES NOT** live on a farm.

Growing Plants

To grow tomatoes, you need to plant the seed, water it, pick the tomato, and eat it. Look at the pictures below and write 1, 2, 3, and 4 to put them in order.

True or False ?

Circle the correct answers.

Insects have four legs.
TRUE or **FALSE**

A lion lives in the savanna.
TRUE or **FALSE**

A chicken has hooves.
TRUE or **FALSE**

A plant needs sunlight to grow.
TRUE or **FALSE**

A zebra lives in the forest.
TRUE or **FALSE**

A caterpillar becomes a butterfly.
TRUE or **FALSE**

A cow lives in the ocean.
TRUE or **FALSE**

A monkey can climb a tree.
TRUE or **FALSE**

WHICH WAY TO GO

TO

Games

Maze

Belinda the ballerina has lost her shoe.
Follow the maze to help her dance again.

Hidden Picture

Color the spaces that have stars.
You'll find a plant that smells as good as it looks!

Connect the Dots

Complete the picture by connecting the dots starting with letter **A**.
Color it in any way you like.

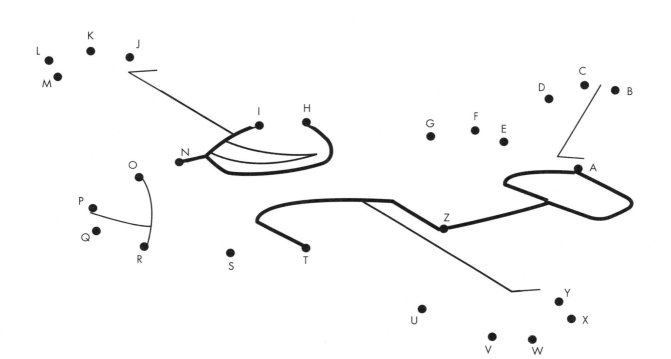

Finding Pairs

Draw a line between the pairs of objects on the beach.

Games

Maze

Paul the plumber can't find the dripping faucet.
Follow the maze to help him find it.

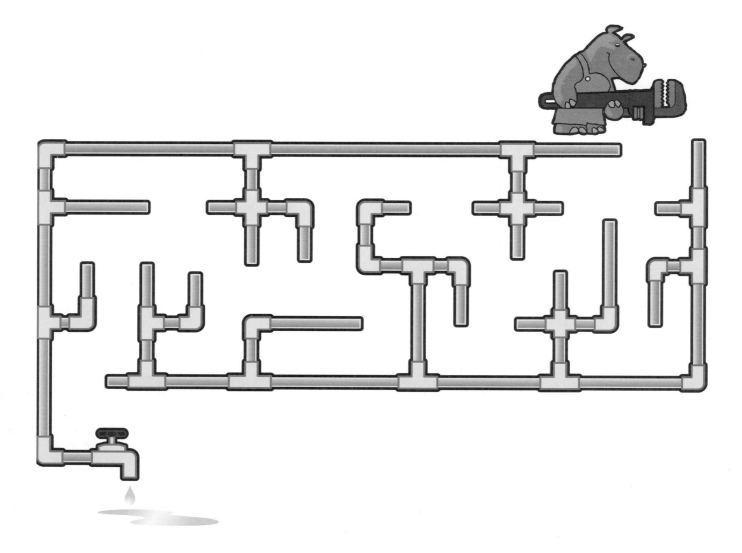

Tic-Tac-Toe

Play this game with a friend. Take turns placing an "x" or an "o" on the grid and the first one to have three in a row (horizontal, vertical, or diagonal) wins!

Connect the Dots

Complete the picture by connecting the dots.
Then color it any way you like.

Hidden Picture

Use the numbers to fill in the hidden picture. Can you also find the diamonds, ovals, and triangles?

red= 1   **blue = 2**

Games

Maze

The orange butterfly needs to find its friends.
Follow the maze to help it get there.

Find a Match

Color the 2 cakes that have the same number of candles.

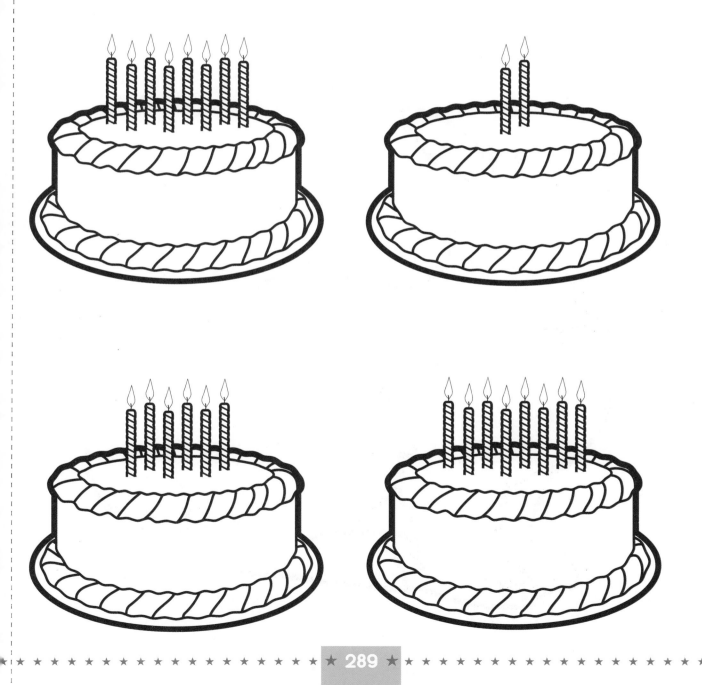

Connect the Dots

Complete the picture by following the numbers 5 to 50, counting by **5**.

25

15

30

10

35

20

5

40

45

50

Follow the Line

Which squiggle line should the monkey follow to get to the most bananas? Trace the correct line with your pencil.

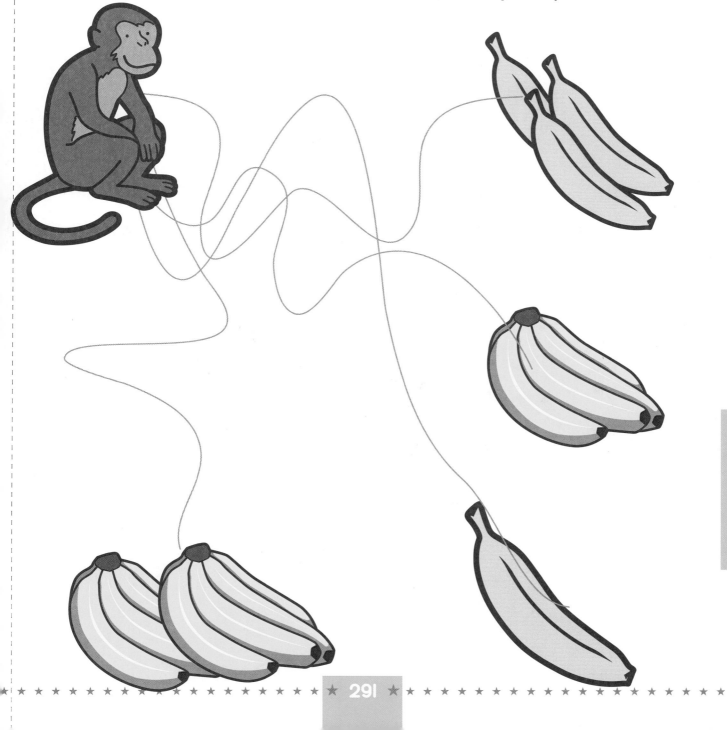

Connect the Dots

Complete the picture by connecting the dots.
Then color it any way you like.

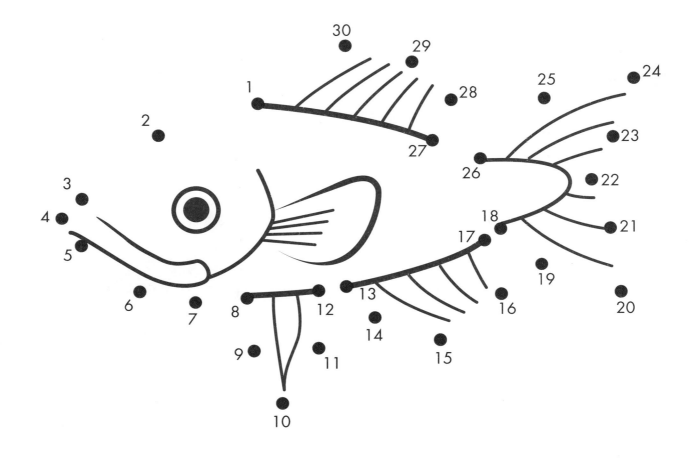

Find the Pattern

Find the patterns in the box and circle them.

Pattern 1: 🐚 🐚 🐚
Pattern 2: ⭐ ⭐ 🐚
Pattern 3: 🐚 ⭐ 🐚

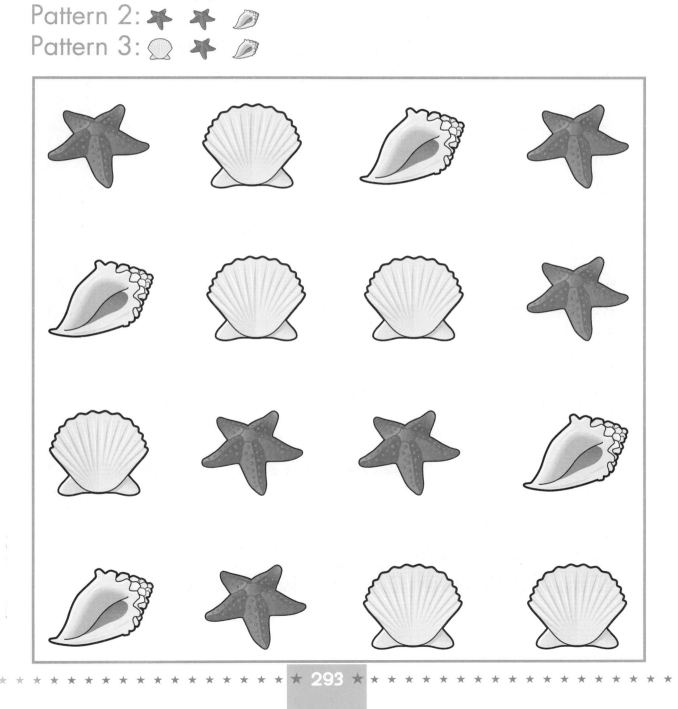

Games

The Maze

Help the dog reach her puppy by following the dog bones in the maze.

Find the Path

Help the duckling find his friends at the pond. Color in the path of flowers to get him there.

Find the Path

Help the crocodile put the money in his register following a path of nickels and dimes.

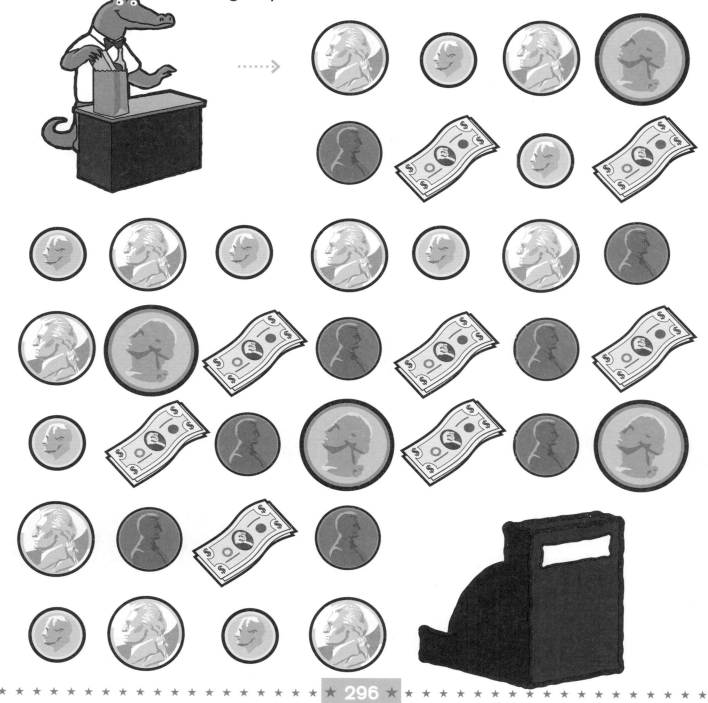

Connect the Dots

Complete the picture by connecting the dots.
Then color it any way you like.

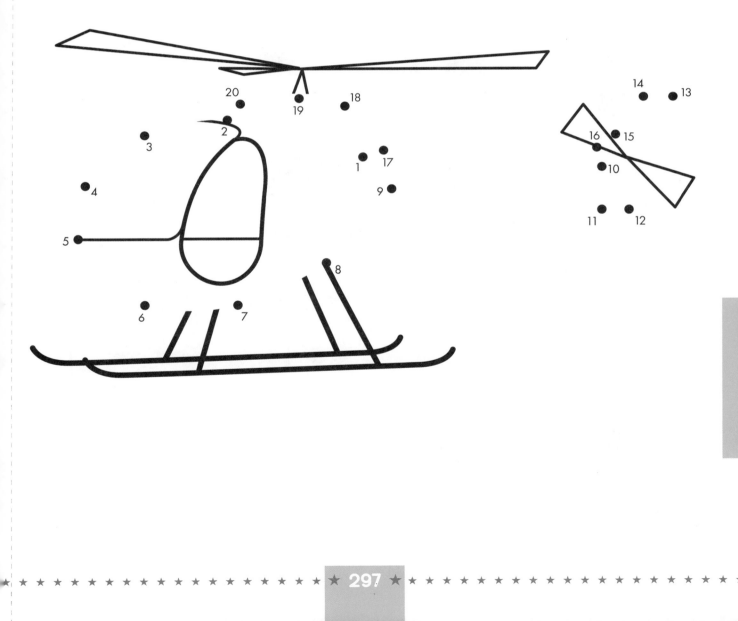

Find the Pattern

Find the patterns in the box and circle them.

Pattern 1:
Pattern 2:
Pattern 3:

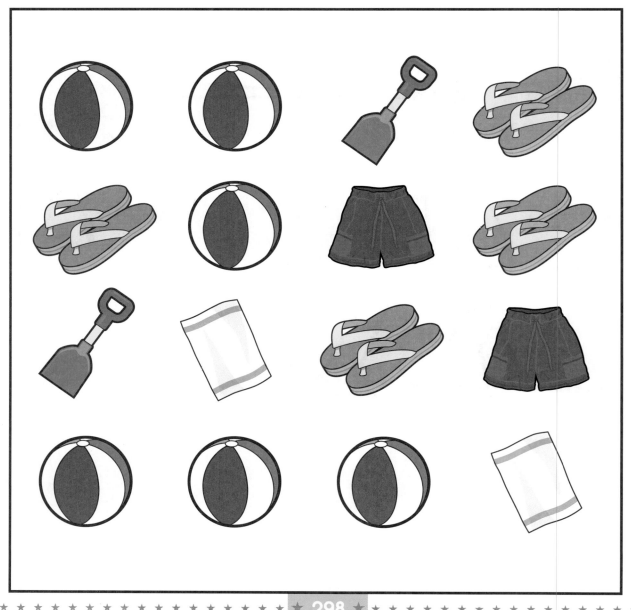

Hidden Picture

Color the spaces that have stars to reveal the hidden picture.

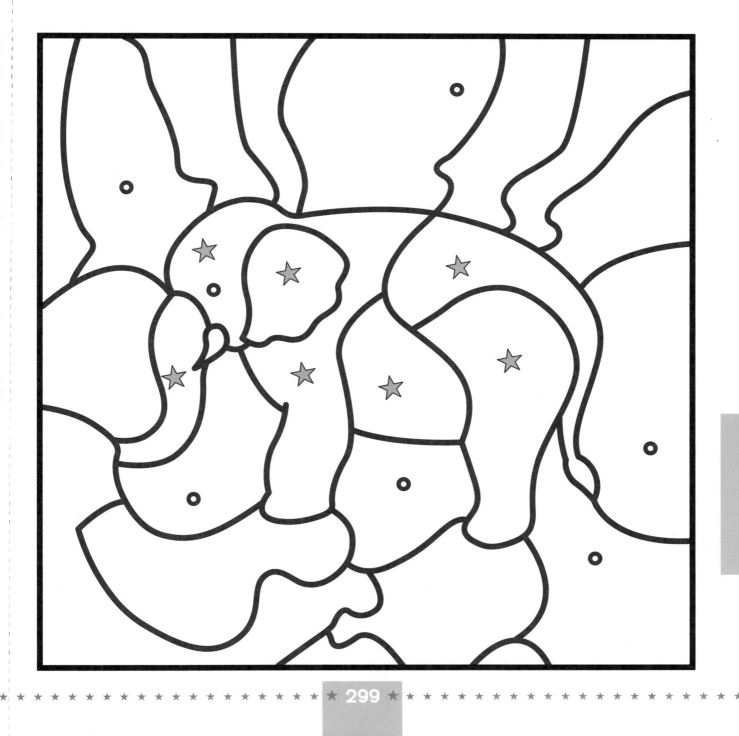

Find the Path

Help the elephant reach his favorite food! Draw a line along the path of triangles and circles to get him there.

Tic-Tac-Toe

Play this game with a friend. Take turns placing an "x" or an "o" on the grid and the first one to have three in a row (horizontal, vertical, or diagonal) wins!

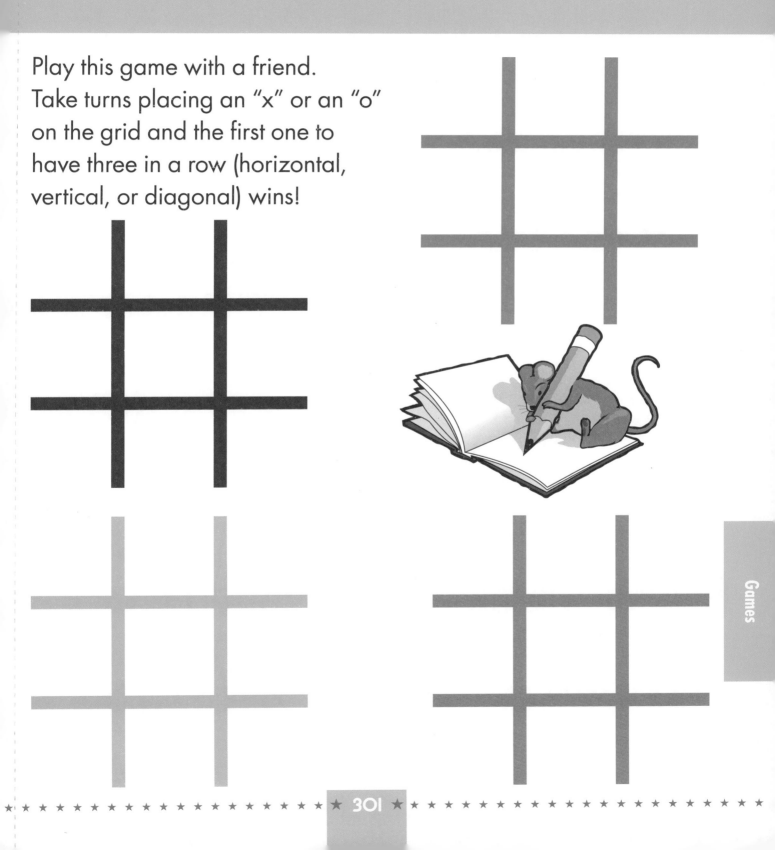

Connect the Dots

Complete the picture by connecting the dots.
Then color it any way you like.

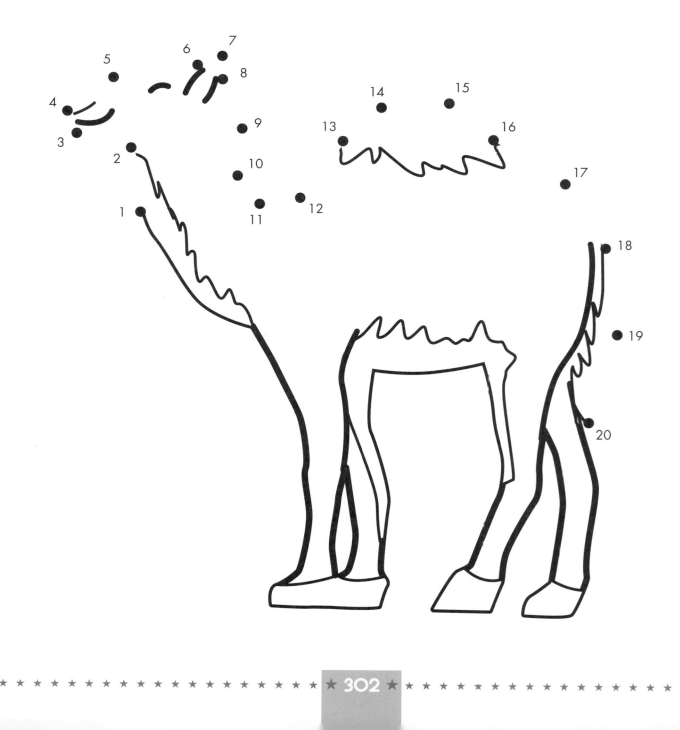

Follow the Line

Which squiggle line should the bunny follow to find his three balloons? Trace the correct line in **green**.

Games

The Maze

Help the builder reach the house he is building. Draw a line following the nails, saws, and hammers reach his house.

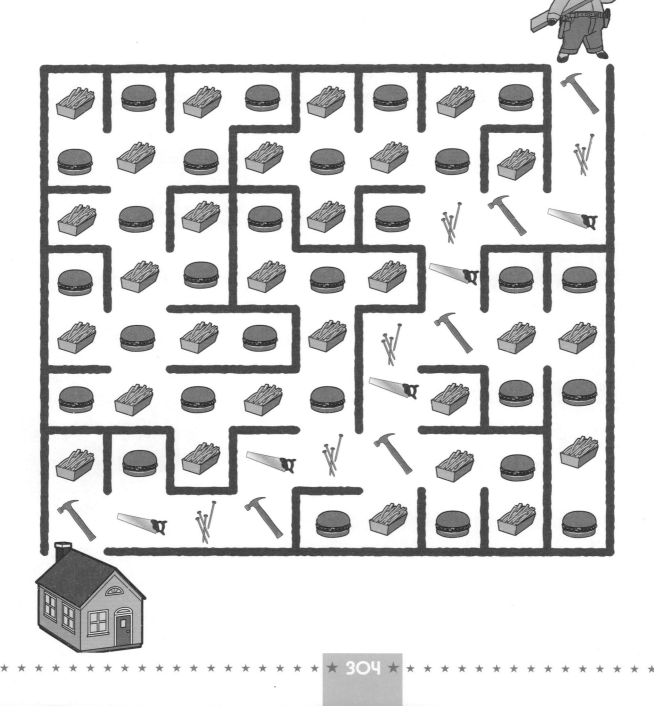

Outdoor Activities

Playground

You need to take turns when you are at the **playground**.
Color in the **playground**.

Bike Safety

If you are riding your bike on the street, which way should the cars be driving? Circle the correct direction below.

Wear a Helmet

Color the objects below where you need to wear a **helmet**.

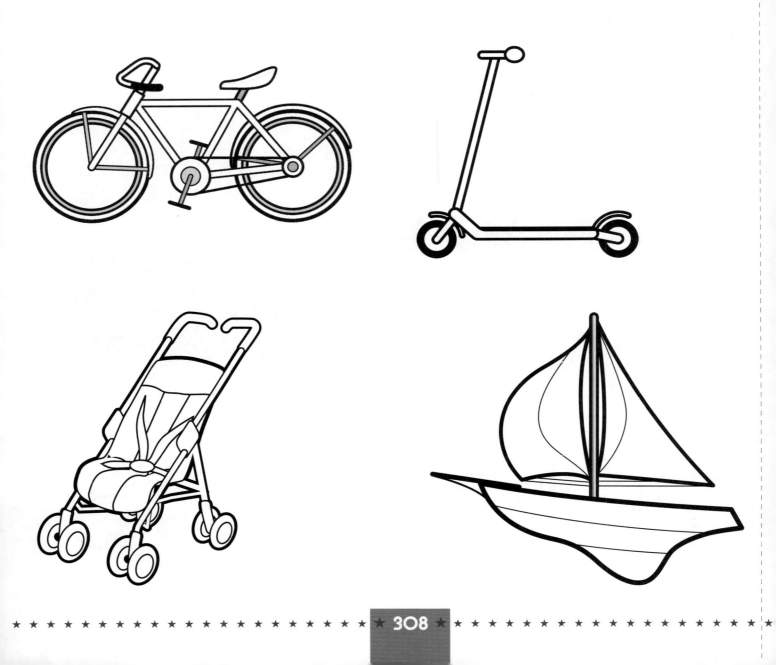

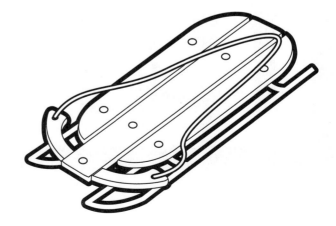

Soccer

Help Sarah the soccer player get to her ball.

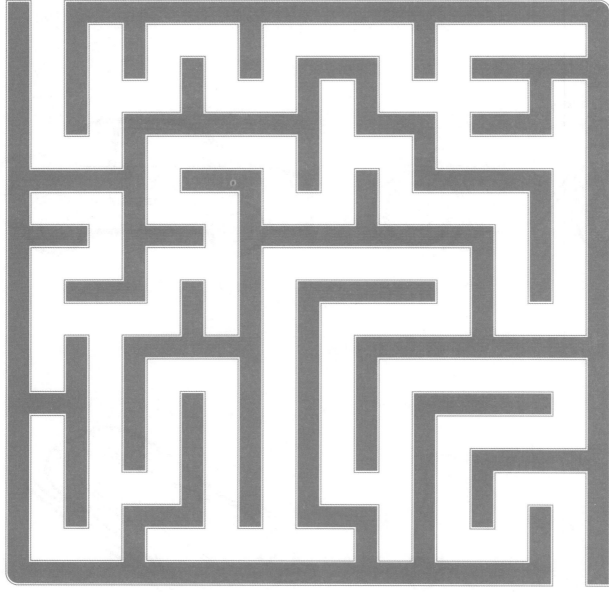

Score!

Different sports use different words when they score.
Match the word with the balls below.

POINT

RUN

TOUCHDOWN

GOAL

Playtime

Circle the activities that you like to play.

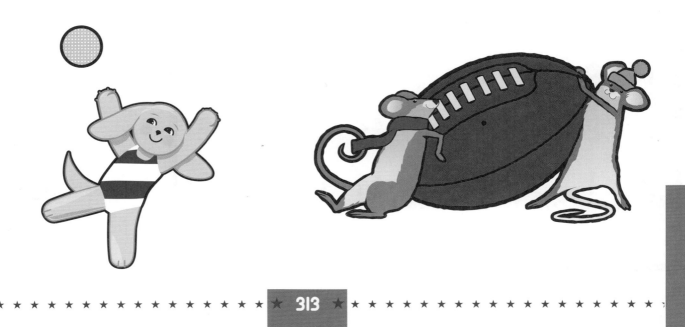

Pool Safety

Never go into the water alone. A grownup should always be with you.

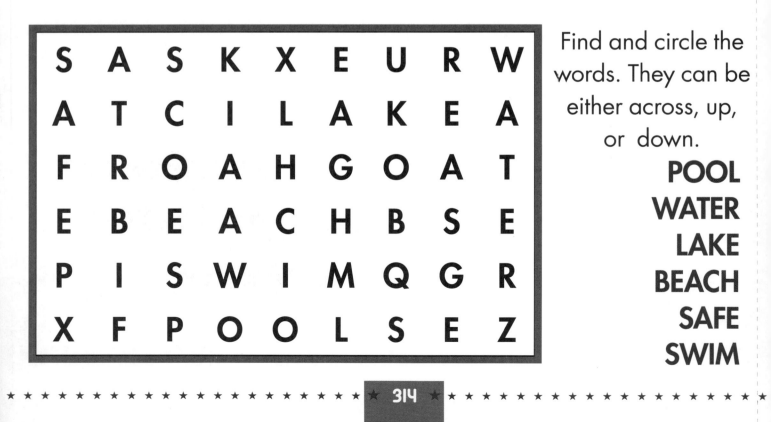

S	A	S	K	X	E	U	R	W
A	T	C	I	L	A	K	E	A
F	R	O	A	H	G	O	A	T
E	B	E	A	C	H	B	S	E
P	I	S	W	I	M	Q	G	R
X	F	P	O	O	L	S	E	Z

Find and circle the words. They can be either across, up, or down.

POOL
WATER
LAKE
BEACH
SAFE
SWIM

Collecting Leaves

Collecting pretty leaves in Fall is fun. Color in one space in the graph for each leaf in its color.

Suggested Reading List

The following is a list of books appropriate for your pre-kindergarten child. We recommend setting aside some time each day to read with your child. The more your child reads, the faster he or she will acquire other skills.

A My Name Is Alice by Jane Bayer

ABC, I Like Me! by Nancy Carlson

All Ready for School by Leone Adelson

Alphabet Under Construction by Denise Fleming

Amazing Graze by Mary Hoffman

Amelia Bedelia by Peggy Parish

Animal Crackers: Nursery Rhymes by Jane Dyer

Antics: An Alphabet Anthology by Catherine Hepworth

Are You My Mother? by Philip Eastman

The Art Lesson by Tomie De Paola

Babushka's Mother Goose by Patricia Polacco

Bear Wants More by Karma Wilson

The Big Dipper by Frankflyn M. Branley

The Big Green Pocketbook by Candice Ranson

Blueberries for Sal by Robert McCloskey

The Cat in the Hat by Dr. Seuss

A Chair for My Mother by Vera B. Williams

Chinese Mother Goose by Robert Wyndham

Click, Clack, Moo: Cows That Type by Doreen Cronin

Clifford the Big Red Dog by Norman Bridwell

Curious George by Hans Augusto Rey

Does the Moon Change Shape? by Meish Goldish

Don't Let the Pigeon Drive the Bus by Mo Willems

Down by the Bay by Raffi

Eensy, Weensy, Spider by May Ann Hoberman

Five Little Monkeys by Eileen Christelow

Frog and Toad Are Friends by Arnold Lobel

Froggy Gets Dressed by Johnathan London

George and Martha by James Marshall

A Giraffe and a Half by Shel Silverstein

The Giving Tree by Shel Silverstein

Green Eggs and Ham by Dr. Seuss

Growing Vegetable Soup by Lois Ehlert

Happy Birthday, America! by Marsha Wilson Chali

Harold and the Purple Crayon by Crockket Johnson

Honeybees by Deborah Heiligman

Horton Hatches the Egg by Dr. Seuss

How Many? How Much? by Rosemary Wells

How the Grinch Stole Christmas by Dr. Seuss

I Know an Old Lady Who Swallowed a Fly by Brian Karas

If You Give a Mouse a Cookie by Laura Joffe Numeroff

If You Take a Mouse to School by Laura Joffe Numeroff

Is It Red? Is It Yellow? Is It Blue? by Tana Hoban

Jumanji by Chris Van Allsburg

Kipper's A to Z: An Alphabet Adventure by Mark Inkpen

A Light in the Attic by Shel Silverstein

Lilly's Purple Plastic Purse by Kevin Henkes

The Little Engine That Could by Watty Piper

The Little House by Virginia Lee Burton

The Little Red Lighthouse and the Great Gray Bridge by Hildegarde H. Swift

Lizards for Lunch-A Roadrunner's Tale by Conrad Storad

Madeline by Ludwig Bemelmans

Make Way for Ducklings by Robert McCloskey

The Man Who Walked Between the Towers by Mordical Gerstein

Math Curse by Jon Scieszka

May Wore Her Red Dress by Merle Peek

Miss Bindergarten Gets Ready for Kindergarten (series) by Joseph Slate

The Mitten by Jan Brett

Mouse Paint by Ellen Stoll Walsh

My First Days of School by Jane Hamilton-Merritt

No, David! by David Shannon

Oh, the Places You'll Go by Dr. Seuss

Olivia by Ian Falconer

One Fish, Two Fish, Red Fish, Blue Fish by Dr. Seuss

One Hungry Monster by Susan Heyboer O'Keefe

Over in the Meadow by John Longstaff

The Paper Bag Princess by Robert Munsch

A Picture Book of Harriet Tubman by David A. Adler

The Polar Express by Chris Van Allsburg

Read-Aloud Rhymes for the Very Young by Jack Prelutsky

Red Leaf, Yellow Leaf by Lois Elhert

School Bus by Donal Crews

The Snowy Day by Ezra Jack Keats

Spot Counts from 1–10 by Eric Hill

Stellaluna by Janell Cannon

The Story of Ferdinand by Munro Leaf

Strega Nona by Tomie de Paola

Sylvester and the Magic Pebble by William Steig

Ten Black Dots by Donald Crews

Ten Seeds by Ruth Brown

Timothy Goes to School by Rosemary Wells

Two Little Trains by Margaret Wise Brown

The Velveteen Rabbit by Margery Williams

GREAT JOB!

_____
name

has completed all the exercises in
this workbook and is ready
for Kindergarten.

_____
date